THE RAJPUT REBELLION AGAINST AURANGZEB

The Rajput Rebellion Against Aurangzeb

A Study of the Mughal Empire in Seventeenth-Century India

ROBERT C. HALLISSEY

UNIVERSITY OF MISSOURI PRESS
COLUMBIA & LONDON, 1977

Copyright © 1977 by
The Curators of the University of Missouri
University of Missouri Press, Columbia, Missouri 65201
Library of Congress Catalog Card Number 77–268
Printed and Bound in the United States of America

Library of Congress Cataloging in Publication Data

Hallissey, Robert C   1941–
    The Rajput Rebellion Against Aurangzeb.

    Bibliography: p. 99
    Includes index.
    1. Mogul Empire—History. 2. Rajputs—History.
3. Aurangzib, Emperor of Hindustan, 1619–1707.
I. Title.
DS461.7.H28   954.02′5   77–268
ISBN 0–8262–0222–5

CONTENTS

ACKNOWLEDGMENTS

I conducted the basic research for this work in India while I was a Language Fellow of the American Institute of Indian Studies. Among the many people who provided assistance to me in India, the late N. R. Khadgawat of the Rajasthan State Archives in Bikaner and Miss Keswani of the Indian National Archives in New Delhi were very helpful and generous with their time. Special thanks also go to the staff of the India Office Library and the Oriental Manuscript section of the British Museum where I completed my research.

I am particularly indebted to the South Asia Center of the University of Missouri and to its director, N. G. Barrier, for his advice and support during my program at the university. I am grateful also to Professors Fredrick Stanwood and Paul Wallace, who made valuable suggestions as readers of my manuscript. A final word of thanks to my wife, Jacquie, who typed the text and provided encouragement and inspiration during its writing.

R.C.H.
Carbondale, Illinois
April 1977

The Rajput princes were the major Hindu allies of the Mughal emperors. For more than two centuries the rajas of northern India served with distinction in the extension of Mughal rule over the subcontinent; from Akbar to Aurangzeb, the Rajputs provided large military forces and a wealth of leadership to the Mughals. Emphasis on this record of service, however, has obscured the process by which the Timurid dynasty adroitly subverted the power of these independent rulers and transformed the Rajputs from powerful adversaries into valuable allies. Concentration on the exploits of the Rajputs as Mughal supporters has also directed attention from the Rajput state itself to the larger empire of which it was a part. Accordingly, little is known about the Rajput kingdom and the internal forces of the Rajput state.

An examination of the Rajput rebellion against the Mughal emperor Aurangzeb provides interesting insights into both of these problems. The succession struggle in Marwar after the death of Raja Jaswant Singh furnishes a valuable example of the dynamics within the Rajput state, and Aurangzeb's intervention in the dispute in Jodhpur illustrates the penetration of Mughal power into a Rajput kingdom.

The traditional accounts of the Rajput rebellion interpret the revolt in a religious perspective. Jadunath Sarkar, the distinguished Indian historian of Aurangzeb's reign, sees the emperor's annexation of Marwar as an attempt to destroy the leadership of Hindu resistance to the imperial policy of persecution.[1] Edwards and Garrett see the alliance of Mewar and Marwar against Aurangzeb as an indicator of a national uprising by the Rajput clans in defense of their country and religion.[2]

1. Jadunath Sarkar, A Short History of Aurangzeb, 1618–1707, p. 160.
2. S. M. Edwards and H. L. G. Garrett, Mughal Rule in India, p. 84.

Although more recent historians have recognized the complexities of Mughal-Rajput relations in the reign of Aurangzeb, the tendency to reduce the Rajput rebellion to a Hindu-Muslim confrontation remains.[3] The polarization of the two great religious communities of the subcontinent has facilitated this view and resulted in a projection of communal differences from the twentieth century into the Mughal period.[4] Although such interpretations possess thematic continuity, they are not consistent with the facts of the rebellion, nor do they advance our knowledge of the Rajput state or our understanding of Mughal imperialism.

In his seminal work on the Mughal nobility, M. Athar Ali suggests that the roots of the rebellion lay in the complexities of the Rajput state itself.[5] A detailed investigation of the rebellion underscores this thesis and points to factors such as clan prestige and the personalities of the Hindu princes as major elements affecting Mughal-Rajput relations. Although religious differences were clearly a determinant in the tone of these relations, Aurangzeb's dealings with the Hindu princes indicate that economic and strategic concerns generally took precedence over religious considerations.

Chapter 1 portrays the contemporary setting of seventeenth-century Rajasthan. Its main focus is on the topography of the area and the impact of this environment on the Rajput mentality. Chapter 2 is an analysis of the Rajput sociopolitical system that examines caste, clan, and lineage in relation to political and administrative organization. Chapter 3 explains the role of the Rajput princes as imperial officers, or *mansabdars*; and Chapter 4 describes the Mughal Empire of Aurangzeb. Chapter 5 surveys the condition of the two leading Rajput states, Marwar and Mewar, on the eve of the rebellion. Chapter 6 considers the death of Raja Jaswant Singh, the impact

3. R. C. Majumdar, et al., *An Advanced History of India*, pp. 494–97.
4. Percival Spear, *A History of India*, 2:56–57.
5. M. Athar Ali, *The Mughal Nobility under Aurangzeb*, pp. 140–41.

of Jaswant's death on the Rathor clan structure, and Aurangzeb's reaction to the maharaja's demise. Chapter 7 traces the extension of the rebellion into Mewar and analyzes the role of the Sisodian ruler, Raj Singh, in the Rajput revolt. Chapter 8 examines the widening dimensions of the war and the alliance of Prince Akbar with the Rajputs, Chapter 9 recounts Aurangzeb's successful campaign against the rebels and the pacification of the Rajput states, and Chapter 10 assays the importance of religion as a factor in the rebellion. The conclusion, Chapter 11, summarizes the causes of the rebellion and analyzes the consequences of the conflict for the Rajput states and for the Mughal empire.

CHAPTER I

THE CONTEMPORARY SETTING

As in modern times, the Aravalli mountains were the central feature of the land dominated by the seventeenth-century Rajput princes. Extending for a distance of nearly five hundred miles from Ahmedabad in the southwest to Delhi in the northeast, the mountains ultimately blend into the great alluvial plain of north India. Delhi Ridge is the last manifestation of the undulating character of the range as it quietly subsides into the Indo-Gangetic plain.

In the south and central parts of the Aravallis where elevation is most pronounced, east-west traffic is almost impossible. In Mughal times all movement in this direction occurred through narrow transmountain passes. In the northern part of the range, wide water gaps permit easier contact between east and west, although these openings also serve as corridors for the periodic sandstorms that blow in from the arid western region.

Physiographically, the Aravalli Range divides Rajwarra into two distinct zones.[1] The western area, dominated by the Thar Desert, is dry and sandy and ranks among the hottest regions in India. The inhospitable climate makes agriculture almost impossible, although modern irrigation methods have been adopted somewhat successfully. In Mughal times, however, the only vegetation consisted of the typical scrub plants of the desert that were used for grazing livestock. Significant cultivation occurred primarily in the areas surrounding the towns of Bikaner, Jaisalmer, Jodhpur, and Nagore. By utilizing wells these cities had access to the water table that exists

1. I have used the Rajasthani word *Rajwarra* to avoid the anachronism of using Rajputana or Rajasthan, the phrases used for the land of the Rajputs during the British and independent periods, respectively.

throughout much of Rajwarra. Although physiographically and climatically separate, this arid western zone is considered part of the Indo-Gangetic plain.[2]

The Eastern Plains zone of Rajwarra, which lies south of the Aravallis, alternates between sloping plateau and monsoonal river basin. This land is more hospitable because rainfall is more plentiful and the soil more alluvial than in the north. The Aravalli Range acts as a barrier to the shifting sands from the western region so the land is more arable, but agricultural production is marginal because the lack of a dependable water supply hampers the development of anything but subsistence farming. The physiographic structure and relief of the Eastern Plains zone is quite different from the western region of Rajwarra and, in fact, the area is more closely related to the Vindhya highlands of the Deccan or the central plateau region of the subcontinent.[3]

The great physiographic and topographic variation within Rajwarra has presented formidable obstacles to the political unity of the region. Immediately before the Mughal conquest of India, the area was divided into innumerable independent principalities. The ruggedness of the terrain permitted easy defense against external invaders, and many petty kingdoms flourished in the security of their mountain or desert fortresses.

Occasionally, however, an invader, such as the Mughals, who possessed awesome military power subdued the entire region by exploiting the political divisions that the physiographic environment had spawned. While the natural fragmentation of the region fostered the proliferation of princely states, it also engendered a parochial outlook that ultimately proved fatal to many of the principalities. Even in the face of a common enemy the princely states could not unite. Clan rivalry and personal jealousies between the respective rulers prevented political alliance and made the princely states easy

2. V. C. Misra, *Geography of Rajasthan*, p. 23.
3. Ibid.

Map 1. Seventeenth-Century India

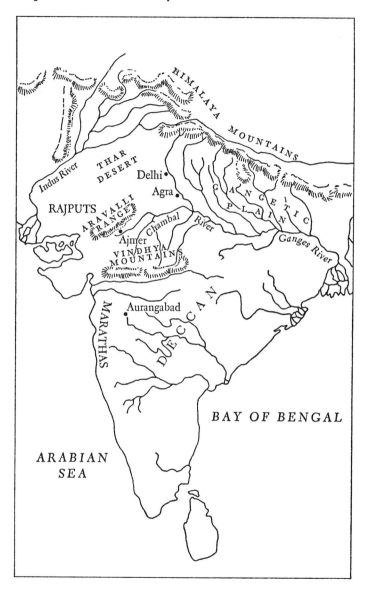

prey for an ambitious invader. Indeed, some chieftains co-operated more readily with an outside power than with their fellow Rajputs. This intense concern with individual fortune, rather than with communal welfare and the general well-being of the Rajputs as a distinct group, ultimately helped the invaders reduce the Rajputs to a position of secondary importance. Only those rajas who cooperated with the conquering power maintained their positions, and even their independence was severely curtailed.

In mid-seventeenth century the number of Rajput princes had decreased sharply as petty rajas were absorbed into the Mughal empire or were annexed by more powerful Rajput states. By Aurangzeb's reign there were three major Rajput kingdoms—the Kachwaha Rajputs of Amber, the Rathors of Marwar (Jodhpur), and the Sisodias of Mewar (Udaipur). The territory that each clan controlled changed constantly, depending on the strength of the respective ruler and on his relationship with the Mughal emperor. At the time of Aurangzeb's accession in 1658, Rajwarra consisted of the area bounded by Delhi (Shahjahanabad) in the north, by Agra (Akbarabad) in the east, by Malwa in the southeast, by Gujerat in the south, and by Multan in the west.

The Mughals had incorporated Rajwarra into the imperial province (*subah*) of Ajmer about 1560. The *Ain-i-Akbari* records that the province measured 168 *kos* (+84 miles) from the dependencies of Amber in the east to Jaisalmer in the west and 150 *kos* (+75 miles) from the northern extremities of Ajmer to Banswara in the south.[4] These boundaries approximated the limits of the Rajput state in Aurangzeb's time, although the emergence of a strong Rajput state at Bikaner in the early seventeenth century probably extended the northern border closer to Ganganagar.

The subah of Ajmer was of great importance as a source of revenue for the Mughals. Although precise statistics on the

4. Abu Fazl-i-Allami, *Ain-i-Akbari*, 2:273.

Map 2. Seventeenth-Century Rajwarra

contributions of the Rajput states to the imperial treasury are not available, Irfan Habib's calculations of the assessed land revenue for the province from 1595 to 1709 suggest that the subah was one of the richest in the empire.[5] Besides sub-

5. Irfan Habib, *The Agrarian System of Mughal India, 1557–1707*, p. 328.

stantial taxes on the produce of the land, the province also contributed important minerals to the Mughals. The *Ain-i-Akbari* relates that zinc and copper mines were located in the province and that the subah also produced large quantities of salt and marble.[6] A contemporary account from Aurangzeb's time also confirms the importance of the mines to the Mughals.[7]

Rajwarra was also a major link in the commerce between the inland cities of Delhi and Agra and the western seaports. Jean Baptiste Tavernier, a Frenchman who traveled extensively in western India in the early seventeenth century, noted that there were two routes connecting Agra with Surat. The western route ran through Rajwarra while the eastern one passed through Malwa. Although merchants using the western route were more vulnerable to the raids of bandits and the financial demands of the Rajput princes, they generally preferred this passage because the monsoons that rendered the road through Malwa impassable had little or no effect in the arid regions of the Rajput kingdoms. Although Malwa was impenetrable for about two months in the rainy season because of flooded rivers and streams, the western route presented no such climatic obstacles to the passage of trade and commerce.[8]

The transit duties that the Rajputs imposed on goods passing through their kingdoms were particularly vexatious to the Mughals. All of the emperors from Akbar to Aurangzeb issued imperial orders (*farmans*) prohibiting the levying of such taxes, but it seems that their decrees were never enforced. In 1633 Peter Mundy, a factor of the English East India Company, complained to the London authorities about

6. Abu Fazl, 2:273.
7. "Waqaya-i-Ajmer, 1678–80," no. 13, "Events of Ajmer."
8. Jean Baptiste Tavernier, *Les Six Voyages de J. B. Tavernier . . . en Turquie, en Perse et aux Indes,* 2:45. Tavernier's memoirs provide a first-hand account of the commercial routes of central and western India in the last half of the seventeenth century.

the high rate of taxation exacted by the Rajput chiefs on goods going from Agra to Ahmedabad.[9] Similar complaints were voiced by another agent of the company in 1648.[10] The taxes apparently were assessed on Mughal goods as well, since one of the imperial newswriters (*waqa' i nawis*) in Ajmer also complained of the Rajput duties.[11]

The roads connecting the imperial cities with the western ports were relatively good. The Agra to Ajmer link of the western route was tree lined and dotted with roadside inns for the comfort of travelers. In the sixteenth century Akbar had improved the road and built many edifices and castles along the way.[12] Although these roads were still probably little more than cleared pathways, they did facilitate the movement of traffic through Rajwarra. Francois Bernier notes that the trip from Agra to Ajmer (a distance of about 230 miles) took only seven or eight days.[13] William Finch, an early English traveler in India, mentions a similar journey for the trip from Agra to Chitor (a distance of about 300 miles).[14]

Military as well as commercial traffic required a substantial network of roads through Rajwarra. The Mughals frequently sent armies into Rajput territory to intimidate recalcitrant rajas, and the Rajput chiefs were expected to provide immediate troop support to the Mughals upon request. Another

9. Peter Mundy, *Travels in Asia, 1630–34*, p. 278.
10. W. Foster, ed., *The English Factories in India, 1646–50*, pp. 192–93.
11. *Waqaya-i-Ajmer*, nos. 15, 16.
12. Abdul Qadir Badauni, *Muntakhab-al-Tawarikh*, 2:173.
13. Francois Bernier, *Travels in the Moghul Empire, 1658–1668*, p. 86. Bernier was a Frenchman who served both as physician and adviser to the Mughal court during his residence in India from 1658 to 1670. He was an eyewitness to many of the events that he relates in his memoirs. Bernier traveled throughout the empire with the imperial entourage, and his observations on the roads and commercial routes are considered accurate and authoritative.
14. William Finch, *Travels of William Finch, 1608–11*, p. 170.

factor that favored the development of a good road system
was the movement of pilgrims through Rajwarra. Cambay and
Surat were the two great ports of embarkation for Mecca, and
both cities were connected to north India through Rajwarra.

In addition to being a main commercial corridor to the
western ports, Rajwarra was also an avenue of access to the
Deccan. As noted earlier, the eastern zone of Rajwarra is
part of the Vindhya highlands, and through the plains of Mewar all of central India was open to the Mughals. Strategically
then, as well as commercially, Rajwarra was of prime importance to the Mughal rulers.

In the Mughal period the key to the control of Rajwarra
was the city of Ajmer. Situated at the approximate midpoint
of the Aravallis, the city was centrally located relative to the
loci of Rajput power—Jodhpur, Udaipur, and Amber. Ajmer
offered a commanding approach to the plains on either side
of the Aravallis, and the Mughals early realized the significance of the city for imperial expansion. Akbar annexed the
city about 1561, and his successors continued to use it as a
base of military operations. By the seventeenth century, the
city had also become an administrative center. Akbar's son,
Jahangir, made the city his capital for almost three years,[15]
and Sir Thomas Roe, the first English ambassador to the
Great Mughal, attended the imperial court (*darbar*) at Ajmer in 1615.[16]

By stationing a strong garrison at Ajmer, the Mughals attempted to maintain the isolation of the Rajput chieftains.
The physiographic features of Rajwarra provided a natural
separation of the Rajput states, and the Mughals, by locating
their provincial headquarters at Ajmer, sought to capitalize on
the parochial mentality that this isolation bred. The primary
concern of the Mughals was the prevention of an alliance between the Rajput states. The continued occupation of Ajmer

15. Jahangir, *Tuzuk-i-Jahangiri*, p. 340.
16. Sir Thomas Roe, *The Embassy of Sir Thomas Roe*, p. 84.

and the natural fragmentation of the region prevented such a coalition from becoming a reality. Only in the reign of Aurangzeb would this policy of isolation be endangered by the alliance between the Rajputs of Mewar and Marwar.

CHAPTER II

THE RAJPUT STATE

Kinship and Political Structure

The distinctive feature of the Rajput political system in the Mughal period was the interrelationship of clan affiliation and land control. In his early analysis of the Rajput polity, James Tod describes this connection as feudal.[1] Although the Rajput pattern of landholding possessed certain features that were analogous to the European model from which Tod drew so heavily, the system also displayed certain unique characteristics that could not be understood when approached with ideas formulated from the European experience with feudalism.

The clan was the most significant element in the Rajput political system. Each of these agnatic groups constituted a ruling elite who, by dint of their military prowess, controlled the political power and the territory within the state. In effect, a Rajput kingdom was a conquest state created by the exercise of military power as each clan asserted preeminence for its chief and predominance for itself by right of occupation.

In each Rajput kingdom the governing authority resided in the chief, or raja, of the dominant clan who was either the military commander who had directed the initial conquest of the territory or his nearest legitimate descendent. The raja was the highest officer in a hierarchy of vassals of varying rank, each subordinate to his immediate superior and ultimately to the clan chieftain. The relative position of each Rajput vassal in the hierarchy depended upon the size of his estate, which was determined by the vassal's relationship to

1. James Tod, *Annals and Antiquities of Rajputana*, 1:153.

the raja, by loyalty to the clan, or by military skill. Each vassal had customary military, economic, and social obligations to his overlord; failure to meet any of these responsibilities would jeopardize his estate.[2]

Although a clan established itself by the use of raw military power, its control would not have endured without the legitimizing effect of the Indian social system. The classical division of society into four castes—priest, warrior, merchant, and peasant—provided a hierarchical social structure that was predisposed to government by a conquering elite.

The Rajputs emerged as the premier warrior caste in India around the seventh century A.D. Their precise origin is unknown, but epigraphic evidence suggests that they were part of the Aryan peoples who invaded the subcontinent shortly after the collapse of the Gupta empire.[3] Certain Indian scholars assert that indigenous elements within the subcontinent also succeeded in establishing claims to Rajput status.[4]

A clan could be called Rajput if it established its right to rule, perpetuated its control through a dynasty, and traced its genealogy to the warrior (*kshatriya*) caste of vedic tradition. Members of the clan would then claim a degree of relationship to some heroic ancestor who possessed leadership and charisma. The Guhilots, or Sisodian clan, of Mewar provide an interesting example of this process. Although acceding to power in the fourteenth century, the clan projected its Rajput ancestry back to 1000 B.C., to Rama, the kshatriya prince of the Ramayana, the ancient Hindu epic.[5] Each clan member believed that he was ultimately related to Rama, and members of the ruling family are known to have maintained in-

2. The vassal even faced confiscation of his territory upon default of his obligations. See Raja Ajit Singh to Dayal Das, 10 March 1710, "Kharita Basta," no. 99.

3. B. H. Baden-Powell, "Notes on the Origin of the Lunar and Solar Aryan Tribes and on the Rajput Clans."

4. See for example D. R. Bhandarkar, "The Guhilots."

5. G. N. Sharma, *Social Life in Medieval Rajasthan*, p. 21.

tricate genealogies (*vanshavalis*) that traced the clan lineage
back to antiquity.[6]

By the seventeenth century the internal structure of the
Rajput caste was one of clearly defined lineages based on clan
affiliation that demonstrated each clan's origin from a heroic
founder and each individual's position within his clan. Only
the ruling houses in Rajwarra would dare assert a claim
stretching into antiquity, but the rich martial tradition of
the Rajput clans permitted nearly every member of the hierarchy to claim a relationship with some heroic progenitor.

Certain structural features within the Rajput social system
contributed to the maintenance of this identification by the
clans with the ancients. The Rajputs of the seventeenth century were an endogamous group that considered itself separate
from other Indian castes. Marriage outside of the warrior
caste meant the forfeiture of caste membership. In addition,
since each clan member was ultimately the descendant of
some common ancestor, marriage was also prohibited within
the framework of one's clan.

The existence of branches (*shakhas*) within a clan also
perpetuated a clan consciousness among the Rajputs. Collateral lines of a given clan considered themselves equal to
the direct descendents of a heroic ancestor. Only the title
of raja, and possibly the size of the holdings, differentiated
the ruling family from the junior branch of a clan. Lineages
of branch members were meticulously maintained,[7] since the
legitimacy of a claim to the throne was a major criterion for
the selection of a new ruler.

Polygyny was a third factor that contributed to a clan consciousness among the Rajputs. The number of wives that a
Rajput chieftain possessed was usually dependent on his economic status, he could obtain as many wives as his finances
permitted. Jaswant Singh, the majaraja of Jodhpur from 1638

---

6. C. Von Furer-Haimenforf, "The Historical Value of Indian Bardic
Literature," pp. 87–93.
7. T. N. Dave, "The Institution of Bards in Western India."

to 1678, for example, had twelve wives, all of whom were Rajput princesses from clans other than his own, the Rathors of Marwar.[8] Even the lowest Rajput could practice polygyny, however, as long as he was able to support more than one wife. The issue of these polygynous unions were very conscious of their Rajput heritage, since each wife attempted to advance the fortunes of her own child by emphasizing his lineage. Within these polygynous unions, as in Rajput society as a whole, there were competing claims of ancestry and status that perpetuated clan identity and membership.

The political consequences of this clan consciousness were quite significant. Any sense of nation or race that a Rajput possessed revolved around his clan. References to the wider grouping of caste were made only for marital purposes and had little political significance. Loyalties to the caste and interests in the fortunes of the community as a caste were very weak. The primary concern of the Rajput was the advancement of clan interest; within the clan an individual's family was most important. The clan was the source of inspiration and the core of community interests, while the family was the font of responsibility, motivation, and success.

With such a societal outlook it is not surprising that most of the vassals in a Rajput kingdom were kinsmen of the chief. Indeed, the word *vassal* suggests a position of subordination that is not really an accurate description of the relationship between the clan chieftain and his kinsmen because clan members, even on the lowest level of the hierarchy, considered themselves to have the same rights as the raja to rule the kingdom. They were coparceners with the chief to dominion over the soil and to the fruits of the land; and the

8. Kaviraja Shyamal Das, *Vir Vinod*, 1:468. Shyamal Das wrote this three-volume history of Rajwarra under the patronage of the maharana of Udaipur. Written in Hindi, the text incorporates modern research techniques and contains extensive direct quotes from Persian and Rajasthani documents in the private library of the maharana. The work is invaluable both as a history of Mewar and as an account of the other major Rajput states. The Indian National Archives, New Delhi.

raja was superior to his kinsmen only in title to the throne (*gaddi*). Thus, the raja ruled by consent of the clan members, and whenever his power weakened or his competency as a ruler decreased, his kinsmen might rebel and depose him.[9]

To counterbalance the ambitions of his own kinsmen, the raja drew support from the foreign Rajputs in his kingdom. Although these Rajputs were members of the warrior caste and many of them were landholders and vassals of the chief, they were not entitled to participate in decisions affecting the state since they were of a different clan than the ruling family. Because they constituted a service nobility, their fortunes became identified with those of the clan chieftain; consequently, the foreign Rajputs were staunch supporters of the ruling family, and service to the raja in the administration of the kingdom or in its defense became their primary function.[10]

The death of a raja could threaten the hierarchical structure of a Rajput state. Although the principle of primogeniture generally operated within a clan hierarchy, the eldest son did not always succeed to power on the death of the clan chief.[11] A raja might designate a favorite son as his successor,[12]

9. There are many examples in Rajput history of a united nobility acting against a clan leader. Perhaps the most famous is the overthrow of the Sisodian ruler Vikram in 1536. The nobles of Mewar murdered the arrogant and self-indulgent ruler and replaced him with the illegitimate son of the great Rajput leader Prithviraj. See G. N. Sharma, *Mewar and the Mughal Emperors*, p. 53.

10. The best essay on the utilization of foreign Rajputs and other castes in the Rajput state is by K. R. Qanungo, "The Role of non-Rajputs in the History of Rajputana."

11. Chandrasen, the ruler of Marwar from 1562 to 1581, was the third son of the Rathor raja Maldeo. The elder brothers of Chandrasen immediately contested his accession and plunged the kingdom into civil war. For a detailed account of the succession struggle between Maldeo's sons, see G. H. Ojha, *Jodhpur Rajya ka Itihas*, 1:333.

12. The practice of a raja nominating as his successor a favorite son or the son of a favorite wife was quite common in Rajput history. Jaswant Singh, for example, the most powerful Rajput ruler during the reign of

or the younger brothers might contest the succession of the eldest son.[13] Rivalry was particularly keen among the direct descendents of a raja. Within the royal household, conflicting claims could be advanced for succession to the gaddi. Often the first wife (*vadi*) would not be the first queen to produce a male heir. When a second or junior wife (*lodi*) became the mother of the heir apparent (*patrani*), a succession struggle was almost certain to occur.[14]

The accession to power by a minor also produced a power struggle among competing factions of the hierarchy. Each sept, or family, within the clan was anxious to advance its territorial holdings and its standing within the clan. The turmoil that attended the accession of a young prince to the throne provided the opportunity for an expansion of personal or family interests by the other members of the clan. Rajputs who were close to the center of power competed for control of the throne through the regency, and clansmen whose interests lay outside the court attempted to extend their holdings by annexation of crown lands.

The most fascinating example of the self-interest of the Rajput clansmen is the succession dispute following the death of the great Rathor ruler Jodha, the founder of the city of Jodhpur. After the demise of their father in 1489, Jodha's sons vied for positions of power within the clan hierarchy. Two of the raja's heirs competed directly for control of the throne,[15] while three other brothers attempted to improve their own situations by expropriating crown territory and establishing independent kingdoms. The most successful of the latter was

---

Aurangzeb, was the younger son of Gaj Singh, the raja of Marwar. Gaj Singh selected Jaswant over his elder brother because the ruler of the Rathor clan was extremely fond of Jaswant's mother. Jaswant had also ingratiated himself to his father. See Das, 1:829.

13. Ratan Singh, the eldest son of the Sisodian ruler, Rana Sanga (1508–1528), was deposed by a coalition of his younger brothers. See G. N. Sharma, *Mewar*, p. 43.

14. G. N. Sharma, *Social Life*, pp. 118–19.

15. Ojha, 1:268.

Bika, whose conquests ultimately developed into the auton-
omous Rathor state of Bikaner.[16]

The competition and rivalry between various septs within
the same clan cannot be overstated. The animosity and antagonism between clansmen extended even to the battlefield.
Soldiers in the field obeyed only those commands issued by
the raja, a royal prince, or the leader of their sept; a Rajput
warrior would rather accept defeat or death than the orders
of an officer from a rival family. Perhaps the most famous
example of this intraclan rivalry is the defeat of Maharaja
Jaswant Singh at the battle of Dharmat, where factionalism
among his Rathor clansmen resulted in the defeat and flight
of the raja's forces.[17]

The ultimate strain on the Rajput political system was the
death of a raja who had failed to produce a male heir. When
this situation occurred, all the fissiparous forces within the
Rajput state came to the fore. The wives of the late chieftain
submitted conflicting claims to his estate, each element within the hierarchy attempted to stake out a larger share of the
clan land, and collateral and junior branches of the clan vied
for political power. The dangers of a raja dying without an
heir were sometimes avoided by adoption. A raja could designate as his heir a member of the junior branch of the clan,
but this procedure frequently only added another element
to the succession dispute.[18]

A vacancy on the throne catalyzed all of the centrifugal
elements that operated within a Rajput state. Normally, the
raja was able, by force or by intimidation, to subordinate
individual and sept interests to the general good of the clan.
His effectiveness as a ruler depended on his ability to main-

16. Mahinot Nensi, *Khyat*, 2:198.
17. Jadunath Sarkar, *A History of Aurangzeb*, 2:361.
18. Chapter 6 examines in detail the civil strife in Marwar following
the death of Maharaja Jaswant Singh, who failed to produce a surviving
male heir by the time of his demise in 1678.

tain a delicate balance between communal welfare and personal ambition. The Rajput state therefore was a composite of corporate interest and individual prestige within the framework of a clan hierarchy. As ruler of the state and as head of the lineage, the raja presided over a sociopolitical system that reflected the military character of the warrior caste and the distinctive features of the Rajput clan organization.

Administrative System

Even though a succession struggle suggests conflict within the ruling elite of the hierarchy, no element of Rajput society was left unaffected by a battle for control of a throne. Each clansman possessed a retinue of servants and retainers that cut across caste lines and extended down to the lowly peasant (*shudra*). Brahmans, artisans, merchants, and cultivators were all dependent on the Rajput for security and sustenance, so that a change in the status or territory of a Rajput automatically affected their fortunes also. This interdependence between a Rajput and his retainers existed for all members of the warrior class, from the top of the clan hierarchy to the most distant Rajputs within the lineage. Clan membership entitled a Rajput to share in the political power, but the clansman maintained his poistion in the hierarchy through the loyalty and support of his retainers. This reliance on non-Rajput elements as support groups was most pronounced in the central administration of the Rajput kingdom.[19]

In contrast to the Rajput sociopolitical system, which reflected the clan hierarchy, the administrative organization of the Rajput state consisted almost entirely of non-Rajput

19. The general illiteracy of the warrior caste and the traditional Rajput disdain for the practical affairs of government also enhanced the importance of non-Rajput elements in the administration of the state. See Susanne Hoeber Rudolph, "The Princely States of Rajputana: Ethic, Authority and Structure."

elements that had no blood relationship to the raja.[20] This civilian administration served, in effect, as a check on the ambitions of the raja's kinsmen. The ruler used the administrative machinery to monitor the political and ecnomic aspirations of his kinsmen and, whenever a clansman arrogated to himself privileges and functions not consistent with his status in the clan hierarchy, the entire weight of the Rajput social structure, activated by the civil administration, was brought to bear against the ambitious kinsman.

As head of the administrative structure a raja exercised complete authority over the internal affairs of his state. His chief non-Rajput officer, the *pradhan*, functioned as a prime minister and was subordinate only to the raja. The pradhan supervised the distribution of land within the kingdom and the fullfillment of obligations that the clansmen owed the raja. No grant of land from the raja was valid unless certified by the signature of the pradhan. Similarly, the fiscal and military responsibilities of the vassals were not officially met until acknowledged by the pradhan.[21]

The *diwan* supervised the financial and revenue departments of the kingdom. He was responsible for the assessment and collection of taxes in the Rajput state; all collections and payments of state funds passed through his office. The diwan, like the pradhan, usually came from the brahman or merchant castes. Both officers were appointed directly by the raja and both had the support of the throne behind their decisions.

The *bakshi* was the paymaster in the Rajput state. He certified the salaries of nobles and clansmen and paid the military commanders. In wartime his office was of critical importance,

20. A Rajasthani proverb summarizes the Rajput attitude toward the appointment of kinsmen to administrative posts: "Make your brother your minister (*pradhan*) and lose your kingdom." See Qanungo. p. 110.

21. Besides these specific responsibilities, the pradhan was usually familiar with the other branches of Rajput administration. See "Haqiqat Bahi," no. 37, p. 162.

since the loyalty of clansmen to their raja often depended on payments from the bakshi for military services.

The *kotwal* was a fourth administrative officer within the Rajput state. He supervised weights and measures in the kingdom, was responsible for law and order, secured the roads against thieves and bandits,[22] and regulated the prices and transit of commercial goods within the state.

By the seventeenth century, the bureaucratic structures of the three major Rajput states, Amber, Marwar, and Mewar were quite similar in name and function. Slight variations in titles did occur,[23] but in each of these Rajput kingdoms the administrative machinery was directly responsible to the raja. The similarity of bureaucratic structure in the respective Rajput states reflected the growing intimacy between the rajas and the Mughal empire. With the single exception of the pradhan, the Rajput rulers patterned their administrative organizations almost exclusively on the Mughal model.[24]

The coterie of administrative officers assembled by the raja constituted an interest group similar in status to the alien Rajputs. Because the civilian administrators, like the foreign clans, were directly dependent on the raja for appointment, they were strong supporters of the ruling family. Since the administrative officials served the raja rather than the state, they were particularly vulnerable to a change in the clan leadership; nonetheless, they exercised considerable influence and power within the clan hierarchy, and they constituted another element to be reckoned with in the event of a vacancy on the throne.

Because the administrative structure was composed of non-Rajputs, clashes between civil administrators and members

22. Man Kavi, "Raj Vilas," canto 2, folio 39, verse 131, Saraswati Bhandar Library, Udaipur.

23. Ibid., folio 33, verses 67–72. Man Kavi refers to the pradhan in Mewar as the *mantri pravar*.

24. For a detailed discussion of the Mughal impact on the Rajput states, see G. N. Sharma, *Social Life*, pp. 348–69.

of the clan hierarchy were quite common, with each group attempting to expand its influence at the other's expense. Decisions about clan policy frequently hinged on the amount of support that a particular clansman could generate among his kinsmen. The prestige of the royal court and its administrative officers was not easily challenged, however, particularly since clansmen often delighted at the diminution in power or status of an ambitious Rajput from a rival sept.

For administrative purposes each Rajput kingdom was divided into territorial regions (*sarkars*). Each sarkar in turn was subdivided into clusters of villages (*parganas*).[25] The village was the smallest administrative unit and the basis of all land grants made by the raja to his nobility. Although all the land in the kingdom was considered common property, the raja, as head of the clan, conferred title and assigned members of the clan hierarchy the right to collect taxes. These territorial grants (*jagirs*) entitled the Rajput noble to collect land revenue and other taxes within a particular area. The size of the jagir given to a Rajput noble depended on his relationship to the raja or on his service to the ruling family. Generally, the amount of assigned territory reflected the status of the clansman within the hierarchy.[26]

Each *jagirdar* (holder of a jagir) duplicated the central administrative structure within his holding so that the jagir became an administrative microcosm of the Rajput state. Pradhans, diwans, bakshis, and kotwals abounded in these petty principalities. The separation of the civil administration from the ruling hierarchy was maintained even in these small holdings. Anxious to preserve their power, the jagirdars, like the rajas, delegated responsibility much more readily to civilian authorities than to their own kinsmen. The ambitions

25. The Rajput rulers also patterned their territorial administration after the Mughal example. See Parmatma Saran, *Provincial Government of the Mughals, 1526–1658*, pp. 1–38.

26. The fiscal and military responsibilities of the jagirdar are examined in detail by P. D. Pathak, "Feudalism in Rajputana."

and aspirations of clansmen posed an equal threat to raja and jagirdar.

The existence of a civilian administration independent of the clan structure provides valuable insights into the nature of the Rajput political system. Rajput reliance on support groups outside of the warrior caste suggests that the state was more a conglomerate of competing interests than a community of kinsmen united by a common purpose. Above all else, the Rajput was a warrior whose main purpose was to advance his individual prestige in relation to his fellow kinsmen. His willingness to die in battle was prompted not by an overriding loyalty to clan or country, but by a desire to increase his status within the lineage. This concern over individual fortune frustrated the growth of a wider national identity and guaranteed the continuance of internecine jealousy within each Rajput clan.

Because the civil administration centered around the personality of a particular ruler, the Rajput kingdom had only limited potential as a viable political entity. Since the retainers and administrative officers who clustered around a Rajput ruler shared the same fate as their patron, an adverse change in the raja's fortunes or his removal from the leadership of the clan hierarchy automatically resulted in a new administration. This bureaucratic instability and political particularism of the clan membership produced a sociopolitical system that was incapable of developing an allegiance broader than the boundaries of clan loyalties. The clan-state of seventeenth-century Rajwarra, therefore, represented a political organization of competing and often conflicting interests presided over by a raja whose position as clan chieftain testified to his ability to balance the many disparate elements within the Rajput state.

CHAPTER III

THE RAJPUT PRINCES AS IMPERIAL MANSABDARS

The Mughal conquest of northern India in the sixteenth century had significant consequences for the Rajput political system; Mughal rule drastically altered the traditional pattern of interdependence between the rajas and the clans. Although the Rajput political structure pitted a raja against his kinsmen, the chief of a clan ultimately depended on the nobility for the continuance of his rule.[1] The Mughal conquest introduced a new element into this relationship; prior to the Mughals the raja had measured support by alliances generated within the clan system. Mughal rule permitted the raja to go outside the clan hierarchy to strengthen his claim to power. The enormous resources that the Mughals controlled were a valuable reserve that the chieftains could utilize in order to intimidate ambitious kinsmen. By employing Mughal power, the rajas became far more autocratic in their relations with the clan hierarchy and less cautious in maintaining the delicate balance of interests within the Rajput states.

Mughal influence on the Rajput polity was most evident in the area of succession. Frequently a Rajput raja would avoid a succession dispute among his sons by having his heir designate formally recognized by the Mughal emperor.[2]

1. A Rajasthani maxim best summarizes the traditional power relationship within the Rajput state: " रिउमत्त गाधिग तिके राजा—the support of the nobles determines the raja." See Kaviraja Shyamal Das, *Vir Vinod*, 1:807–8.

2. The rajas were particularly careful to obtain imperial recognition when they nominated a favorite son as successor. Gaj Singh, the maharaja of Marwar (1619–1638), for example, bypassed his eldest son

The new raja could subsequently accede to the throne (*gaddi*) without having made the traditional promises of munificence and favor to his kinsmen. In gaining the throne, as well as in exercising their princely powers, the Rajput rajas were becoming increasingly independent of the clan hierarchy.

By offering the rajas an alternate power base, the Mughals enabled the Rajput rulers to ignore the traditional claims of the clan membership for a share in political power. The rajas acknowledged the suzerainty of the emperor and promised tribute and troop support to the Mughals in their conquest of the subcontinent. In turn, the Mughals recognized the special position of the Rajput rulers in the empire and accorded them many honors consistent with their new dignity.[3] This redefinition of the Rajput power structure in Mughal terms exploited the very fabric of Rajput society. By offering the rajas the opportunity to increase their power at the expense of the clan hierarchy, the Mughals appealed to the Rajput rulers' intense ambition of advancing their individual prestige and fortune.

The Mughals appreciated the value of the rajas as allies. The Timurids, like other Muslim dynasties before them, had swept into the subcontinent from the northwest. Drawn to India by the promise of pillage and plunder, the Mughals possessed little knowledge of the land they conquered. As foreigners, the Mughals had to rely on indigenous elements for help in governing their new empire, and the Rajput rajas became a major factor in their successful rule of the subcontinent.

Akbar, emperor from 1556 to 1605, was the first Mughal to recognize the importance of alliance with the Rajputs.

---

for his favorite, Jaswant Singh. By securing the approval of Shah Jahan for his heir designate, Gaj hoped to avoid a succession dispute after his death. See ibid., pp. 828–29.

3. For a detailed discussion of the Mughal system of awards and distinctions, see Radhey Shyam, "Honors, Ranks and Titles Under the Great Mughals."

He initiated policies that were designed to conciliate the Rajput chieftains and to establish the foundations for permanent rule of the subcontinent. Akbar gained their support by acknowledging the authority of the rajas in the internal affairs of their kingdoms and their positions as heads of the clans.[4] As long as the policies of the rajas did not affect imperial affairs, they were free to operate unrestrained within their respective states. Clan affairs were the domain of the raja, and his decisions were seldom questioned by the Mughal emperor.

Akbar also sought to guarantee the allegiance of the Rajput rulers by taking Rajput princesses as brides. The rajas willingly furnished their daughters to the Mughals, since these matrimonial affiliations gave them an additional claim to imperial resources.[5] Traditionally, the Rajputs married within the warrior caste, but the opportunities for increased power and prestige that marriage with a Mughal presented were not easily overlooked.

The mansabdari system of the Mughals offered the Rajput rajas another opportunity to expand their influence outside the clan structure. Appointment as a military commander (*mansabdar*) entitled the holder to draw a salary from the imperial treasury for his personal rank (*zat*) and to maintain a specified number of troops (*sawar*) that could be placed in service to the emperor.[6] In lieu of salary, the Mughals frequently granted the mansabdar a territorial grant (*jagir*), which included revenue that usually exceeded the remuneration received directly from the imperial treasury. Payment by

4. Abu Fazl-i-Allami, *Ain-i-Akbari*, 1:323, 348, 421, 509.

5. The Rathor Rajputs of Marwar and the Kachwaha Rajputs of Amber in particular provided many princesses to the Mughals. Ibid., p. 510.

6. For a detailed discussion of the zat and sawar components of the mansabdari system, see M. Athar Ali, *The Mughal Nobility under Aurangzeb*, pp. 38–43. Because of the special position of the Rajputs in the imperial service, the zat and sawar were usually the same. Unless noted otherwise in the text, reference to mansabdari appointment means an identical zat and sawar.

jagir had the further advantage of permitting the raja to re-
ward his loyal supporters by subdividing his territory's revenues
among them.

Mansabdars who held the rank of commander of one thousand or more troops were considered nobles (*amirs*) of the
empire and accorded positions of honor at the imperial court.
All of the major Rajput rajas were amirs. By accepting appointment in the mansabdari system, the Rajput rajas gained
formal recognition of their titles by the emperor and received
confirmation of their possession of clan land. The rajas acknowledged the suzerainty of the Mughals and placed their
services at the disposal of the crown in return for imperial
recognition.

The mansabdari system was mutually beneficial to Rajput
and Mughal. The raja gained an opportunity to increase his
personal power by imperial appointment. With Mughal authority behind him a raja could act with impunity toward
the clan hierarchy; no longer did he have to conciliate a disgruntled kinsman or calculate his moves in terms of their
impact on the clan structure. The raja, backed by Mughal
authority, could defy a Rajput sept, or even a branch (*shakha*),
of the clan and consolidate his own power at the expense of
both elements of the lineage. In short, the mansabdari system
provided the raja with a unique opportunity to advance his
individual interests outside of the traditional support and
alliance groupings of the Rajput clan hierarchy. Imperial appointment was a revolutionary innovation in Rajput government and in the hierarchical relationships within the clan.

The Mughals also derived many benefits from Rajput
participation in the mansabdari system. As conquerors, the
Mughals appreciated the importance of military power,
and they recognized the value of the troops and leadership
that the rajas provided.[7] By absorbing the Rajputs into the

7. The Mughal emperors rarely undertook a major military campaign
without Rajput support. Perhaps the leading example of the confidence
that the Timurids placed in their Rajput allies was Aurangzeb's appoint-

mansabdari system, the Mughals pacified one of their major opponents and bound the fortunes of the rajas to those of the imperial dynasty. The Mughals, through the mansabdari system, built a tributary relationship with the rajas that provided revenue and military support without the onus of administrative expense. The emperors assigned the chieftains to pay a specified amount of tax, which was paid from their jagirs, and delegated collection responsibilities to the rajas. The Mughals also gained ultimate power over the Rajputs by obtaining the right to officially confer the clan throne on members of the lineage.[8]

By the seventeenth century the impact of the mansabdari system on the Rajput sociopolitical structure was unmistakable; the independence of the raja from the clan hierarchy had revolutionized the traditional Rajput system. The power of the clan and the importance of the lineage had declined, centralization of authority had replaced the dispersion of power among Rajput kinsmen, and the raja had consolidated his power and relegated clansmen to positions of minor importance within the state. In addition, the civil administration had displaced the clan hierarchy as the central organ of the state, and its members were wielding more power than any Rajput clansman.[9] In structure, the Rajput kingdom in-

---

ment of Jai Singh of Amber as commander of the imperial forces against Shivaji in 1664. The Muslim emperor apparently had no fear of an anti-Mughal alliance between the two great Hindu warriors. See Mirza Muhammad Kazim, *Alamgirnama*, p. 878.

8. The Mughals formally recognized a new raja by the conferral of the right to rule (*tika*). Tika legitimized the new ruler and certified that he was acceptable to the Mughals. Akbar was the first emperor to use tika to settle a succession dispute in a Rajput state. By recognizing the accession of Mota Raja Udai Singh (1583–1595) to the throne of Marwar, Akbar ignored Rajput custom and the decision of Rao Maldeo, the former raja, who had disinherited Udai Singh, his eldest son. See "Jodhpur Rajya ki Khyat," 1:97.

9. One consequence of imperial service for the Rajput rajas was frequent absence from their kingdoms. The raja usually delegated complete

creasingly resembled the organization of the Mughal empire;
the titles and functions of the civil administrators (*diwan*,
bakshi, and *kotwal*) were identical to their counterparts in
the imperial administration. Through matrimonial alliances
and the mansabdari system, the Mughal emperors had isolated the Rajput chieftains from their traditional power base
and weakened the ties between the clan hierarchy and the
Rajput political structure.

Even though a Rajput chieftain accepted imperial appointment as a mansabdar, his primary intention was not service
to the emperor, but rather the pursuit of personal power. The
rajas generally regarded the mansabdari system as they had
the clan, as an organization useful for the consolidation and
advancement of their own personal interests. The raja was not
bound by loyalty or allegiance to a higher authority, nor did
he recognize the wider political dimension of the empire in
which he participated. He attempted to use imperial office,
as he had the leadership of the clan, for self-aggrandizement
and profit. Parochial and personal interests were the moti-
vating force of the Rajput rajas whether they operated with
the support of the clan or the Mughal empire. Personal prestige, and not clan or imperial interests, was the primary objective of the Rajput chieftains.

The best example of this approach to the mansabdari system is Raja Jaswant Singh, the ruler of the Rathor state
of Marwar, who held power in Jodhpur from 1638 to 1678.
Jaswant's accession to power provides valuable insights into
the nature of the Rajput state and its relationship to the
Mughal empire. Jaswant was the younger son of the Rathor
ruler Gaj Singh. His elder brother, Amar, had been disin-

---

responsibility for state affairs to the pradhan and other civil administrators, who were much more trustworthy than his own kinsmen. In Marwar, the civil administration became so powerful that its offices tended
to become hereditary. See Susanne Hoeber Rudolph, "The Princely
States of Rajputana: Ethic, Authority and Structure," pp. 23–24.

herited by Gaj Singh, who had obtained imperial approval in 1638 for his selection of Jaswant as his heir.[10]

As noted earlier, primogeniture was not an inviolable principle of Rajput polity. Legitimacy was a significant factor, but the ability to rule was equally important. The approval of the Mughal emperor was a third element in the accession to the gaddi, and at the time of Gaj Singh's death in 1638 it seemed to be the most important consideration. Jaswant's first action after the death of his father was to march to Agra where he obtained formal recognition as ruler (*tika*) from Shah Jahan on 25 May 1638.[11] The fact that he was a minor at the time of his father's death and the presence of his brother Amar at the imperial court certainly prompted Jaswant's concern over imperial recognition, yet it is rather curious that the young king never bothered to obtain clan approval of his accession until nearly two years after he had ascended the throne; his formal coronation at the fort of Jodhpur and his installation as head of the clan did not occur until March of 1640.[12]

Further evidence of the declining power of the clan and of the growing influence of the Mughals in the internal affairs of Marwar was the appointment of administrative officers by the emperor. Shah Jahan twice appointed treasurers (*diwans*) in Jodhpur during Jaswant's minority. At the time of Jaswant's accession, the emperor appointed Rajsingh Kumpawat of Asop as diwan, and three years later he appointed Rathor Mahesdas, a member of the main line of the Rathor clan, to succeed the deceased Rajsingh.[13]

Although he assumed the right of imperial appointment in Marwar, Shah Jahan was careful to cultivate the goodwill of the Rathor nobility. At the time of Jaswant's accession, he presented robes of honor to the Rathor clansmen attending

10. Das, 1:829.
11. Abdul Hamid Lahori, *Badshahnama*, 2:92.
12. "Jodhpur Rajya ki Khyat," 1:196.
13. Lahori, 2:122.

the imperial court,[14] and his appointment of Mahesdas as
diwan can be seen as a concession to clan interests. It should
be noted, however, that one of Jaswant's first actions upon obtaining his majority in 1641 was to replace Rathor Mahesdas
with the more loyal and less ambitious Mertia Gopaldas, who
was not a member of the clan hierarchy.[15] Mahesdas revolted
against the young raja, but a royal army under the command
of Mahinot Nensi eventually subdued the rebel clansman.[16]

Jaswant Singh's early selection of a civil administrator over
a Rathor kinsman indicated the new raja's attitude toward
the clan hierarchy. Jaswant planned to undermine the traditional control by the Rathor nobility of the Jodhpur throne
by building a base of power that would be independent of
the clan structure. Service with the Mughals would then permit him to organize a loyal civil administration ultimately
supported by the authority of the emperor.

Jaswant succeeded in raising his mansab from an initial
command of four thousand to one of seven thousand at the
time that Shah Jahan was deposed by his son Aurangzeb in
1658,[17] but he had a rather undistinguished career as a military commander. He did serve Shah Jahan in campaign from
Qandahar to Jaisalmer and attain the title of maharaja in
1654,[18] but he never established himself as a leader on the
battlefield. Perhaps Jaswant's most heroic action was accepting command of the imperial forces against Aurangzeb in the
succession dispute among the sons of Shah Jahan in 1657–
1658. Jaswant's mansab was accordingly raised to commander
of seven thousand and he was designated governor (*subahdar*)
of Malwa—two positions never before accorded a Rajput.[19]

14. Bankidas, *Bankidas ki Khyat*, p. 29.
15. Bisheshwar Nath Reu, *Marwar ka Itihas*, 1:214.
16. "Jodhpur Rajya ki Khyat," 1:250.
17. Shah Nawaz Khan, *Maathir-ul-Umara*, 1:754–56.
18. Muhammad Salih Kambu, *Amal-i-Salih*, 3:180.
19. Muhammad Kazim states that Jaswant held a position of distinction among the Mughal nobility. See Muhammad Kazim, p. 32.

Aurangzeb's rout of the imperial forces under the command of Jaswant Singh was an ignominious defeat for the Rathor raja. After his humiliating defeat at Dharmat, Jaswant tried to salvage some prestige by quickly allying with Aurangzeb. The Mughal prince had assumed the regnal title of "Alamgir" (World Conqueror) shortly after his victory. The ruler of Marwar paid homage to the new emperor on the banks of the river Sutlej in September 1658,[20] but this expression of loyalty was subsequently belied by additional alliances with Aurangzeb's brothers, Shuja and Dara. Jaswant also conspired against Alamgir by reaching an agreement with the Mughal's enemy in the Deccan, the Maratha leader Shivaji.[21] When it became apparent that no combination of his enemies could defeat Alamgir, Jaswant petitioned the emperor for pardon and was reinvested with the throne of Jodhpur.[22]

Jaswant Singh emerged from the Mughal war of succession with his title and mansab intact, but Alamgir was well aware of the value of such a fickle ally. Initially, Alamgir appointed Jaswant to important posts such as subahdar of Gujerat,[23] but once the new emperor was secure in power he demoted the Rathor raja in the imperial service. Jaswant's last days were spent as a garrison commander (*thanadar*) of Jamrud, a Mughal military outpost in Afghanistan. He had held this position three times since 1671, and he died at Jamrud on 10 December 1678.[24]

Jaswant's tergiversation during the Mughal war of succession and his career as a mansabdar were representative of

20. Ibid., p. 183.

21. Francois Bernier, *Travels in the Moghul Empire, 1658–1668*, p. 187.

22. Aqil Khan Razi, *Waqiat-i-Alamgiri*, p. 42.

23. Alamgir twice appointed Jaswant as subahdar of Gujerat, in 1659 for a term of three years and again in 1670 for one year. See Ali Muhammad Khan, *Mirat-i-Ahmadi*, 1:244, 276–77.

24. There is some confusion about the date of Jaswant's demise, but I have accepted the date mentioned by Saqi Mustad Khan, *Ma'asir-i-Alamgiri*, p. 174.

the Rajput approach to alliance. Expediency and not principle guided the rajas in their relations with the Mughals and with their own kinsmen. Desire for individual aggrandizement and personal power superceded the claims of clan and empire on the loyalties of the Rajputs. Political survival and the desire to expand individual power at the expense of the clan were the motives that prompted the rajas to ally with the Mughals, but the Rajput rulers were as incapable of making a lasting commitment to the Mughals as they were of making one to their own kinsmen. Their ultimate fate was to be absorbed by the empire that they claimed to serve.

CHAPTER IV

THE MANSABDARI SYSTEM
UNDER AURANGZEB (1658–1678)

Although the Rajputs constituted the largest Hindu element within the mansabdari system, they represented only
a small part of the Mughal officialdom; foreign-born Muslims
comprised the largest single component of the Mughal nobility. During the twenty-year period from 1658 to 1678, more
than two-thirds of the Muslim Mughal nobility came from
central or western Asia.[1] Turanis (Turkish-speaking Muslims
from central Asia), Iranis, and Afghans were the major ethnic
groups within this foreign Muslim nobility.

The percentage of non-Indian Muslims employed by the
Mughals remained almost constant from Akbar to Aurangzeb.
In his analysis of the mansabdars listed in the *Ain-i-Akbari*,
Moreland states that nearly 70 percent of the Muslim nobles
in the Mughal service were foreign born,[2] and this was also
the approximate percentage of foreign Muslims in the mansabdari system during the first twenty years of Aurangzeb's
reign.[3]

Aurangzeb's main task during his early years in power was
to find positions for his Muslim and Hindu officers. The young
prince had won the war of succession by virtue of his ability
as a military commander, and he resolved to strengthen his
hold on the Mughal throne by proving that his regnal name
Alamgir (World Conqueror) was justly deserved. Alamgir
believed that a policy of territorial expansion would provide
employment for his military commanders and enable the

1. M. Athar Ali, *The Mughal Nobility under Aurangzeb*, p. 35.
2. William H. Moreland, *India at the Death of Akbar*, pp. 69–70.
3. Ali, p. 35.

crown to make additional jagir appointments to a nobility that was quickly becoming saturated with talented but restive soldier-administrators.

In the first decade of his reign, however, Alamgir's attempts to expand the territorial limits of his empire resulted in costly failure. In 1661 the emperor dispatched a force under Mir Jumla, the governor of Dacca, to invade the kingdoms of Kooch Behar and Assam.[4] The rulers of these states, which were located on the northeastern extremities of the empire, had seized Mughal territory during the war among the sons of Shah Jahan.[5] When Alamgir emerged victorious from the succession dispute, he had vowed to recover the imperial possessions and to punish the eastern rulers for their audacity.

In November 1661, Mir Jumla reached the capital of Kooch Behar after overcoming minor resistance and forced the ruler there, Bhim Narain, to surrender his capital and to cede his entire kingdom to the Mughals.[6] Shortly after the annexation of the Kooch Behar territory into the Mughal lands (*khalsa*), the imperial forces prepared to move further eastward against Assam, which was ruled by the Ahoms, a Mongoloid people who had migrated into eastern India from Upper Burma. The Ahoms offered stiff resistance to Mir Jumla, but the Mughals finally gained control of the Assamese capital in March 1662.[7]

The Mughals realized an enormous booty from these eastern campaigns,[8] but in reality the imperial forces won a pyrrhic victory because the rainy season began before they could withdraw to Dacca. The victors experienced enormous losses due to the lack of food supplies, the prevalence of malaria, and the night attacks of the enemy.[9] Mir Jumla him-

---

4. Muhammad Hashim Khafi Khan, *Muntakhab-ul-Lubab*, 2:130.
5. Saqi Mustad Khan, *Ma'asir-i-Alamgiri*, p. 40.
6. Khafi Khan, 2:142.
7. Ibid., p. 157.
8. Ibid., pp. 130, 157.
9. Shihab-ud-Talish, "Fathiyah-i-Ibriyah," p. 80.

self succumbed to the hardships of the inhospitable climate
in March of 1663.[10] His successor, Shayista Khan, managed to
salvage some territorial gains from these campaigns, but the
Mughals paid a high price in men and material for their victories. The opportunities for imperial appointment that resulted from these conquests were minimal, since few members
of the nobility would accept jagirs or offices in the enervating
climate of the eastern frontier of the empire.

Mughal expansion in the south proved equally unsuccessful.
Jai Singh, the Rajput mansabdar from Amber, had detached
the Maratha leader Shivaji from his alliance with the ruler
of Bijapur; nonetheless, the Rajput general had failed to reduce the power of Bijapur, which remained the strongest
Muslim kingdom in the Deccan. According to the terms of
the Treaty of Purandar, Shivaji agreed to furnish a contingent
of Maratha troops for the Mughal assault against Bijapur.[11]
Late in 1665 Jai Singh, commanding the combined Mughal
and Maratha forces, attacked the Muslim kingdom, but he
could advance no closer than within twelve miles of the
Bijapuri capital. Recognizing the futility of the campaign,
Alamgir relieved Jai Singh of his command in 1666 and
ordered the Rajput ruler to return to the imperial court.[12]

The emperor had barely recovered from the failure of the
Deccan campaign when messengers brought word of a major
uprising by the Afghan tribes in the northwest. The Yusufzais,
the Afridis, and the Pathans, who inhabited the mountainous
regions along the Afghan border, perennially defied Mughal
authority and exercised a quasi independence in their mountain kingdoms. Occasionally the tribes would attack Mughal
outposts or harass the valuable caravans that traveled between central Asia and the Mughal empire. In 1667, however,

10. Mustad Khan, p. 45.
11. The precise terms of the Treaty of Purandar are contained in the
letters from Jai Singh to the emperor. See "Insha-i-Haft Anjuman."
12. Mustad Khan, p. 60.

a chief of the Yusufzai tribe proclaimed himself king and marched in open rebellion across the Indus into Mughal territory.[13] Removed from the safety of their mountain retreat, the Yusufzais were no match for the Mughals. Alamgir ordered the governor of Kabul to send an army of five thousand troops against the rebels and also dispatched a force of nine thousand men from Delhi.[14] Within six months the tribesmen were defeated.

Although the Mughals succeeded in crushing the rebellion, the uprising by the Yusufzais revealed the vulnerability of the imperial forces in the mountainous regions of the northwest. Five years later, in 1672, a much more serious challenge to Mughal authority occurred with the revolt of the Afridis. Acmal Khan, the leader of this warlike people, successfully united all the clans of the Afridis and then gained the support of the Yusufzais and the Pathans with early victories against the Mughals. In 1673 he even managed to close the Khyber Pass.[15]

The Afridi chieftain declared his independence from Mughal authority and asserted his sovereignty by striking coins in his own name. Outraged at the pretensions of Acmal Khan, Alamgir assumed personal control of the campaign against the Afghan tribes, and in June 1674 he arrived near Peshwar to direct military operations against the rebels.[16] Using diplomacy and bribery, the emperor split the ranks of the rebellious Afghans. He remained in the northwest nearly eighteen months, and by the time of his departure in 1676 he had pacified the region.[17] When he left, Alamgir turned over the administration of the territory to Amir Khan, the viceroy of Kabul. The khan secured the area by pensioning the tribal

13. Ibid., p. 61.
14. Ibid., p. 62.
15. Jadunath Sarkar, *A History of Aurangzeb*, 3:228.
16. Mustad Khan, p. 132.
17. Ishwardas, "Fatuhat-i-Alamgiri," folio 69a.

chieftains and paying their kinsmen to patrol the roads that they had once raided.

Even though Alamgir succeeded in reducing the independence of the Afghan chieftains, his campaign in the north-west resulted in no additional territorial gains for the empire. The tribal rulers remained in possession of their lands, which were only nominally part of the khalsa. The mountain chieftains continued to exercise almost complete autonomy over their tribal territories. They acknowledged the suzerainty of the emperor, but they were paid handsomely for their profession of loyalty to him.

The policy of external expansion initiated by Alamgir shortly after his accession to power ended in complete failure: the invasion of Assam resulted in humiliating retreat, and the conquest of Kooch Behar proved largely unprofitable. The campaign against Shivaji in Maharashtra ended in a costly stalemate, and the invasion of Bijapur was an outright disaster. The empire realized no territorial gains as a result of the defeat of the Afghan tribes. Because Aurangzeb had justified his seizure of the throne on the basis of his military achievement,[18] the failure of his expansionist policy was of critical consequence. The Mughal nobility had supported Aurangzeb in the war of succession because the young prince seemed the most capable of Shah Jahan's sons. The defeat of the imperial forces and the elimination of his brothers as rival claimants to the throne indicated, even to those nobles who had opposed him, that their prospects would improve behind the banner of Aurangzeb. However, the debacle of his expansionist policy in the first decade of his reign jeopardized the support of the nobility, since the promotions and increased jagirs that most of Aurangzeb's adherents had expected failed to materialize.

18. Aurangzeb used the legal opinion of Qazi Wahab to support his seizure of the throne. The argument stated that his competence as a military commander proved that he would be a better ruler than his father. See Ali Muhammad Khan, *Mirat-i-Ahmadi*, p. 248.

The basic problem that confronted Alamgir was the lack of suitable lands (*paibaqi*) available for the assignment of jagirs. Without these territorial revenue grants, the entire mansab-dari system would collapse. Although Alamgir had failed to add to the territory that might be placed in jagir, his military campaigns had raised the number and the expectations of the mansabdars in the Mughal service. Realizing the gravity of the situation, the emperor resolved to turn from a policy of external expansion to one of internal consolidation. Accordingly, he decided to reduce the power of the strongest element within the nobility—the Rajputs.

Because of their religion, the Rajputs could be easily isolated from the rest of the nobility. More importantly, they represented a class of imperial officials whose titles and jagirs were disproportionate to the services that they actually rendered to the empire. In order to gain their allegiance during the war of succession, Aurangzeb had promoted the leading Rajput nobles; but during the contest for the Mughal throne and the frontier campaigns the value of the Rajputs as military allies seemed questionable. Jaswant Singh, the Rathor ruler of Marwar, offered his services to the highest bidder during the succession struggle, and his record as a military commander in Alamgir's employ was lackluster. Raj Singh, the head of the Sisodias of Mewar, maintained his traditional aloofness from Mughal affairs, but he readily accepted gifts and increases in his mansab from the emperor. Only Jai Singh of Amber, the ruler of the Kachwaha Rajputs, was of any real value to Alamgir. The Kachwaha raja served with distinction against Shivaji and the Marathas, but his failure in the Bijapuri campaign annoyed Alamgir. As noted earlier, the emperor relieved the Rajput ruler of his command one year before the raja's death in 1667.

Alamgir had hesitated to split the ranks of the Mughal officials, but the failure of his policy of external expansion dictated that he either consolidate his power or risk the loss of his throne. The death of Shah Jahan in 1666 eliminated the threat of a restoration movement; consequently an attack on the nobility could be undertaken with relative impunity. It was possible that some Muslim nobles might object to the divisive effects of such a campaign, but the prospects of increased revenues from seized Rajput lands proved ample incentive for them to endorse the imperial policy of internal consolidation.

Although he decided to reduce the rank and the power of the Rajputs, Alamgir could not risk an open confrontation with the chieftains. With the exception of the Irani element, the Rajputs comprised the largest racial group within the Mughal nobility;[19] they commanded a considerable number of troops, and there were many competent and experienced officers within their ranks. A direct attack on the Rajputs as a group might provoke a general alliance among the various clans, and the emperor, whose image as a military commander was severely tarnished by the frontier fiascos, could not afford to openly challenge any segment of the nobility.

Alamgir chose instead to reduce the power and independence of the leading Rajput chieftains by limiting the number of jagirs that they could hold outside their homelands. Jaswant Singh, for example, on two occasions lost jagirs lying outside his native Marwar.[20] Alamgir also attempted to decrease the number of troops maintained by the Rajput chieftains. For example, at the time of his death in 1667 Jai Singh of Amber commanded a mansab of seven thousand troops; his son, Ram Singh, only received a mansab of four thousand when he assumed his father's office.[21]

Alamgir subsequently allotted to other groups of the Mughal nobility the revenue grants and promotions that might have gone to the Rajputs.[22] The emperor pursued this

19. Ali, p. 35.
20. "Akhabarat-i-Darbar," year 9, pp. 273, 297, 344. Bikaner Collection.
21. Shah Nawaz Khan, *Maathir-ul-Umara*, 2:301–3.
22. Ali, pp. 24, 99–100.

policy of neglect into the second decade of his reign, and it continued to be the official imperial attitude toward the Rajputs at the time of Jaswant Singh's death in 1678.[23]

23. Abul Fazl Mamuri, "Tarikh-i-Aurangzeb," folio 156b.

CHAPTER V

MARWAR AND MEWAR ON THE EVE OF THE RAJPUT REBELLION

Because he was the second son of the previous raja and assumed office without the complete support of his clan, Jaswant Singh, as raja of Marwar, built an effective civilian administration that countered the traditional influence of the clan hierarchy. Early in his reign, Jaswant indicated his intention of becoming independent of clan control: in 1643 he assumed direct responsibility over the affairs of state by dismissing his diwan, who was a Rathor kinsman appointed by the emperor Shah Jahan; and he used non-Rajputs, such as Mahinot Nensi, as military commanders.[1] Jaswant was also successful in reducing the power of non-Rathor elements within his kingdom. The Sindhals and the Hada Rajputs, two groups that resented the Rathor dominance of Marwar, were bribed or coerced into submission.[2]

Jaswant was able to challenge the clan hierarchy by dint of his participation in the mansabdari system; being appointed a commander in the Mughal military system provided him with the dignity of imperial recognition and the backing of Mughal power and wealth. Consequently, a challenge to the raja was not only an attack on a legitimate ruler but also an assault on an imperial servant, and few Rathors were prepared to make such a bold assertion of clan discontent.

The loyalty that Jaswant bought with his munificence was precarious at first, but in time the fortunes of the civil administrators became so intimately connected with those of

1. Bankidas, *Bankidas ki Khyat*, p. 30.
2. "Jodhpur Rajya ki Khyat," 1:247–48; "Waqay Sarkar Ajmer and Ranthambhor," pp. 44, 55–56.

the Rathor raja that their support was unflagging. Jaswant's control over Marwar was largely a result of his success as an imperial mansabdar. The promotions he received and the increasing value of the jagirs and the honors bestowed upon him by Shah Jahan and Alamgir enabled the raja to distribute favors and financial support within his kingdom.[3] His mansab as commander of seven thousand troops was second in importance and size only to those of the royal princes, each of whom held the rank of commander of ten thousand troops. His appointments as subahdar of Agra under Shah Jahan and as governor of Gujerat under Aurangzeb increased his prestige enormously, both within Marwar and within the Mughal empire;[4] he was hailed by contemporaries as the premier noble of the empire and the head of the rajas of Hindustan.[5]

Serving as a Mughal mansabdar also had disadvantages because imperial appointment required prolonged absences from Jodhpur. However, Jaswant could appoint a civil administrator to govern the kingdom without fear of clan reaction. Even in the uncertain times of the war among the sons of Shah Jahan, when it was very doubtful that imperial forces would be available to suppress clan uprisings, the Rathor raja had so reduced the power of the clan hierarchy that he could entrust the kingdom to his non-Rathor pradhan, Sundar Das of Jalor, and leave Jodhpur to fight against Aurangzeb.[6]

Even though appointment in the mansabdari system enabled Jaswant to increase his personal power within Marwar, he became an imperial servant and surrendered his independence and freedom of action to the Mughal emperor. The extent of Mughal power made it difficult for him to do other-

3. Abdul Hamid Lahori, *Badshahnama*, 2:299, 335–36; Mirza Muhammad Kazim, *Alamgirnama*, p. 189; Saqi Mustad Khan, *Ma'asir-i-Alamgir*, p. 5.

4. Lahori, p. 346; Ali Muhammad Khan, *Mirat-i-Ahmadi*, pp. 276–77.

5. Muhammad Kazim, p. 32; Shah Nawaz Khan, *Maathir-ul-umara*, 3:509.

6. "Brij Lal Pancholy," folio 37a.

wise, but working within the imperial structure reduced the proud Rathor raja to little more than a Mughal vassal. Jaswant had to place himself and his troops at the disposal of the empire and was allowed little or no control over his own fate. The Mughals could appoint him to high imperial posts such as governor of a province (*subahdar*) or reduce him and his troops to the status of a border garrison. Perhaps the best indicator of the authority that the Mughals exercised over all of their mansabdars was the passport system (*dastak rahdari*) that required an imperial administrator to obtain Mughal permission before leaving his assigned post. No trip or passage could be undertaken without first procuring imperial sanction.[7]

In addition to losing personal freedom, Jaswant became increasingly dependent on imperial favor. When Mughal power passed from Shah Jahan to Alamgir, the Rathor raja's status, both as the ruler of Marwar and as an imperial mansabdar, was uncertain. Because Jaswant had alternately supported Shah Jahan, Dara, and Shuja against Aurangzeb in the Mughal war of succession, the new emperor questioned Jaswant's value as an ally. In 1659, as if to remind the Rathor chief of his delicate position, Alamgir appointed Jaswant's nephew, Rai Singh, as raja of Jodhpur, deposing the disloyal Jaswant.[8] Shortly thereafter, Jaswant renounced his support of Aurangzeb's opponents and was restored to the throne of Jodhpur through the intercession of Jai Singh of Amber.[9] Alamgir subsequently appointed Jaswant subahdar of Gujerat and finally garrison commander (*thanadar*) of Jamrud in Afghanistan.

By the time of his third appointment in Mughal service, the appointment to Jamrud in 1678, Jaswant had success-

7. The permit (*dastak*) instructed all local officials and other imperial mansabdars to allow the holder to pass through their jurisdictions. For an example of the dastak rahdari, see British Museum, Persian Manuscript Collection, Oriental 26, 140.

8. Muhammad Kazim, p. 326; Bankidas, p. 32.

9. Ishwardas, "Fatuhat-i-Alamgiri," folio 44b.

fully centralized his authority in Jodhpur and reduced the influence of the clan. He had organized a civil administration independent of the clan structure, and he had raised the power and prestige of his kingdom in the empire through participation in the mansabdari system. Jaswant's rank as commander of seven thousand troops and his status as an imperial official forced the Rathor nobility into submission. The Rathor clansmen recognized the futility of rebellion against a raja who ruled with the consent of the emperor. The maharaja's intimate association with the Mughals also precluded any alliance between the Rathor nobility and the emperor, since both Shah Jahan and Alamgir appreciated Jaswant's ability to maintain order in a region that was important for the general stability of Rajwarra.

Nonetheless, by centralizing his power and by ignoring the traditional ties of clan structure Jaswant had alienated many of his kinsmen. An undercurrent of resentment against the Rathor raja permeated the clan and threatened to erupt in open rebellion if an appropriate opportunity were offered. Alamgir astutely perceived this attitude, and his temporary appointment of Rai Singh as successor to Jaswant reminded the maharaja of the deep divisions that existed throughout Rathor society.[10]

Clan ties were never as strong in Mewar as in Marwar. The Sisodian Rajputs of Mewar were politically dominant; they controlled the gaddi, and they never exhibited the exclusiveness and the factionalism that were found in Marwar. The raja of Mewar (*rana*) was able, therefore, to enlist the support of caste and clan elements within the state and consolidate his position without resorting to Mughal power.

10. Jaswant was particularly sensitive about Alamgir's appointment of Rai Singh, since the emperor had overlooked Jaswant's own son, Prithvi Singh. Alamgir's selection of a successor from a collateral branch of the clan alarmed Jaswant and reminded him of his dependence on Mughal power.

Under Raj Singh, who ruled from 1652 to 1680, the prestige of Mewar increased considerably. The Sisodian raja accepted appointment as an imperial mansabdar, but he never willingly participated in the Mughal military system. He always maintained an aloofness from imperial affairs, though he was accorded high honors by both Shah Jahan and Alamgir. Raj Singh never presented himself at the Mughal court, nor did the Sisodian Rajputs ever offer a princess in marriage to the Mughals. It was this independence of action that placed the rulers of Mewar at the fore of the princely houses of Rajwarra.

Raj Singh centralized his control over Mewar by securing the loyalty of all the elements within the state. He drew freely on the talents of his kinsmen and frequently appointed Rajputs from outside his own clan to important posts. The Sisodian raja also employed many non-Rajputs in the affairs of state. Unlike Jaswant Singh of Marwar, the strength of the Sisodian monarch was the complementary support of clan members, non-Sisodian Rajputs, and non-Rajput administrators. The distinctions between these groups in Sisodian society were not as clearly drawn as in Marwar, nor did the rana need to check the ambitions of each group. Raj Singh's main concern as raja was resisting Mughal penetration of Mewar, and the Rajput ruler marshaled all the resources at his command to frustrate imperial attempts to curb his power. Raj Singh indicated his intention of defying Mughal authority early in his reign. In violation of his father's treaty with Shah Jahan, he repaired the walls of the fortress of Chitor.[11] Later he sheltered a kinsman, Garib Das, who had left the Mughal court without permission and then further provoked imperial reaction by appointing Garib Das as his chief adviser.[12] Shah Jahan retaliated by moving against Mewar in September 1654. His commander, Sadullah Khan, destroyed the fort of Chitor and forced the raja to sue for peace. The rana's physician, Govind, was sent to ask pardon from Shah Jahan for his

11. Inayat Khan, "Shah Jahanama," p. 53.
12. Muhammad Hasham Khafi Khan, *Muntakhab-ul-Lubab*, 1:728.

master's acts of defiance,[13] and a treaty was concluded in November 1654.

Raj Singh learned from this early indiscretion and never again challenged Mughal authority so blatantly. Although Shah Jahan demanded that the rana send his sons to the imperial court as a token of submission and also annexed some Sisodian territory, Raj Singh remained firmly in control of Mewar. Except for an attempt to expand his territory during the war among the sons of Shah Jahan, Raj Singh remained at peace with the Mughals for the next twenty-five years. He focused his attention on improving conditions within Mewar by sponsoring public works such as the construction of irrigation facilities and artificial lakes.[14]

In keeping with his policy of drawing from all the factions within his kingdom for service to the state, Raj Singh frequently posted non-Rajputs to the imperial court. In 1679, for example, Garibdas, Raj Singh's chief priest, headed the Sisodian mission to Alamgir's court along with the rana's son, Jai Singh.[15] At this time Raj Singh held the mansabdari rank of six thousand troops[16] even though he never actively served in the cause of the Mughals.

The contrast between the two most powerful Rajput states in the last quarter of the seventeenth century was quite marked. Maharaja Jaswant Singh of Marwar, the premier Rajput noble of the empire, used the power of the Mughals to free himself from the control of the Rathor clan hierarchy. He built a civil administration that was independent of the clan structure and staffed his organization with supporters who were more loyal to him than were his own kinsmen. In centralizing power, however, Jaswant alienated many of his Rathor clansmen who merely bided their time for a chance to dislodge the maharaja and his followers from the gaddi.

13. Sada Shiva, "Raj Ratnakar," canto 10, verses 7–9.
14. Man Kavi, "Raj Vilas," canto 8, folio 102, verses 28–33.
15. Mustad Khan, p. 175.
16. Muhammad Kazim, p. 194.

Many Rathors also resented Jaswant's association with the Mughals and the position of subservience that the maharaja's active participation in the Mughal military system apparently acknowledged.

Although Raj Singh of Mewar also held mansabdari rank, he did not place himself and his troops at the complete disposal of the emperor. The rana of Mewar remained master of his own affairs and used the resources of his clan, his caste, and the non-Rajput element in his kingdom to thwart Mughal penetration of the Sisodian state.

The respective positions of the two Rajput rajas in relation to the clan structure explains this difference in approach to Mughal power. Raj Singh was secure in his hold of the Sisodian throne and was the acknowledged leader and head of state. His kinsmen readily recognized his position as clan leader and their own obligations as his vassals. Jaswant Singh, by contrast, was the second son of the ruler of the Rathor state, and the heirs of his disinherited elder brother disputed his legitimacy. Alamgir's appointment of Rai Singh to the gaddi of Jodhpur after Jaswant's treachery at Khajwa demonstrated that the question of legitimacy was still unsettled even twenty years after Jaswant's accession. The Rathor tradition that all kinsmen had the same rights to the throne as did the raja and the growing power of the civil administration were other factors that were peculiar to Marwar. The explosive nature of these elements within the Rathor state became apparent on the death of Jaswant at Jamrud in December 1678.

CHAPTER VI

THE RAJPUT REBELLION:
MARWAR AND THE RATHORS

The death of Maharaja Jaswant Singh had ominous consequences for the state of Jodhpur. Prithvi Singh, Jaswant's last surviving son, had died of a fever at the imperial court in 1675,[1] and the absence of a direct male descendent almost guaranteed a succession struggle among the collateral branches of the clan. The existence of a strong civil administration added another element to the impending dispute over the gaddi of Marwar.

As soon as the news of the maharaja's demise reached Jodhpur, the Rathor clansmen and the civil administrators took steps to secure their respective positions. The Rathor clansmen stationed at Jamrud were the first to act. Immediately after the death of Jaswant, they instructed the maharaja's ambassador (*vakil*) at Delhi to request that the emperor grant the jagirs of Sojat and Jaitaran to them for their maintenance.[2] Imperial recognition of these traditional holdings would reconfirm the predominance of the ruling sept of the clan and provide a source of income for the officials who were with Jaswant at the time of his death. The Jamrud Rathors also sent instructions to their kinsmen in Jodhpur to cooperate with any imperial officials sent to Marwar.[3] By cultivating a friendly relationship with Alamgir, the Jamrud officials hoped to gain the upper hand over the civil administration through the proven method of allying themselves with the Mughals.

However, few Rathors were willing to concede leadership of the clan to the officials stationed at Jamrud. Shortly after the

1. "Jodhpur Rajya ki Khyat," 1:270.
2. "Waqaya Sarkar Ajmer and Ranthambhor," pp. 90–91.
3. "Brij Lal Pancholy," folio 154a.

news of Jaswant's death spread throughout Marwar, almost twenty thousand clansmen descended on Jodhpur in the hopes of improving their respective situations.[4] One of the leaders of the resurgent clansmen was Rani Hadi, Jaswant's third wife and a princess of Bundi.[5] The queen (*rani*), like the kinsmen of her late husband, was anxious about her future in Marwar, and she appealed to Alamgir to guarantee her safety and inheritance. The emperor replied to the requests of the Rathors by issuing an imperial order (*farman*) stating that he would either recognize the grants and jagirs conferred on the Rathor nobles and officials by Jaswant Singh or convert their assignments to corresponding mansabs in the imperial service.[6]

Aurangzeb tried to conciliate all of the important groups within the clan. He agreed to the proposal of the Jamrud Rathors and granted Sojat and Jaitaran to the ruling family; he also sent a separate farman to the Jodhpur Rathors granting jagirs to those who remained loyal to the empire and assuring them of his support.[7]

The concern of the Jamrud officials over their own future was quite justifiable. The Jamrud party consisted of Jaswant's most loyal kinsmen and administrators, who had risen to power by backing the Rathor ruler in his campaign against the clan structure. The maharaja's death on the Afghan frontier was inopportune for his officers because they were so distant from the center of Rathor power in Jodhpur. They realized, however, that decisions concerning the affairs of Marwar would be made in Delhi, not Jodhpur, so they proceeded to the imperial capital in quest of continued security and position.[8]

Those widows of the late maharaja who were in Jamrud also found themselves in a very delicate situation. Rani Hadi's

4. "Jodhpur Rajya ki Khyat," 1:276; "Waqaya Sarkar Ajmer and Ranthambhor," p. 78.
5. "Waqaya Sarkar Ajmer and Ranthambhor," p. 77.
6. Ibid., p. 144.
7. "Brij Lal Pancholy," folio 16b.
8. Muhammad Hashim Khafi Khan, *Muntakhab-ul-Lubab*, 2:259.

actions in Jodhpur indicated that they too faced strong competition for imperial favor. Since two of Jaswant's queens at
Jamrud were pregnant,[9] it was imperative that they take steps
to safeguard the inheritance of their expected progeny. Their
position was especially difficult because of the Mughal custom
of confiscating all the property of an heirless noble at the time
of his death. The entire estate of a Mughal amir automatically
escheated to the empire at the time of his death and the amir's
territorial holdings were immediately absorbed into the
khalsa. Jaswant's Jamrud widows, like his officers, had only
limited hopes of compensation for their service to the late
maharaja.

Aware of the competing interests at Jamrud and Jodhpur,
Alamgir proceeded very cautiously in establishing his policy
toward Marwar, but several things prompted the Mughal
emperor to take definitive action. The imperial policy of
salary advances guaranteed an indebted nobility, and mansabdars were quite frequently overdrawn on their accounts
with the Mughal diwan. Even by Mughal standards, however,
Jaswant was heavily indebted to the imperial treasury at the
time of his death. As early as 1670–1671, during his first appointment as subahdar of Gujerat, his indebtedness exceeded
several hundred thousands (*lacs*) of rupees.[10] His demotion
from subahdar of Gujerat to thanadar of Jamrud might have
permitted the maharaja to reduce his expenditures, but there
is no evidence that Jaswant Singh settled his account with
the imperial treasury by the time of his death in 1678.

A second factor that prompted Alamgir to establish a definitive policy toward Marwar was the posthumous birth of two
sons to Jaswant at Lahore in February 1679.[11] Because the
Jodhpur Rathors were certain to start an internecine conflict
by contesting the legitimacy of the two princes, who were then
in the control of the Jamrud officials, Alamgir ordered the

9. "Brij Lal Pancholy," folio 153a.
10. Ali Muhammad Khan, *Mirat-i-Ahmadi*, p. 208.
11. Saqi Mustad Khan, *Ma'asir-i-Alamgir*, p. 107.

infant princes brought to Delhi where the question of their
legitimacy would be decided.[12]

Even without the birth of two sons to the late mahajara,
the situation in Marwar was volatile. Jaswant's policy of
centralizing authority and his delegation of responsibility to
civilian administrators had created an undercurrent of discontent among the Rathor nobility, and the sudden death of
the maharaja provided the opportunity for their resentment
to surface. Ishwardas Nagore, a Brahman who held a high
post in the state's administration, noted that at the death
of Jaswant every Rajput household in Marwar prepared to
make trouble and mischief.[13] The explosive nature of the
situation in Marwar was also noted by an imperial servant in
Jodhpur who cautioned the emperor not to allow the Jamrud
Rathors to return to their homeland, since their presence
would only create more disturbances.[14]

Although Alamgir's policy of strong action in Marwar
prevented the outbreak of any large disorders, the Mughal
presence tended to add to the discontent in the state. The
sizable number of imperial appointments made by Alamgir
displaced civil administrators from their positions and swelled
the ranks of those who were ready to create mischief.[15] The
emperor's policy also had the effect of negating the differences
between the administrators and the clansmen, since both
groups were now largely removed from a share in power.
Fortunately for Alamgir, the Rathor clansmen, instead of
seeking an alliance with the disgruntled administrators, de-
voted themselves to the contest for the control of the gaddi.

The Jamrud Rathors left Lahore for Delhi at the end of
February 1679 with Jaswant Singh's infant sons, and they arrived at the imperial capital on 7 April 1679.[16] A week later

12. Ibid., p. 109.
13. Ishwardas, "Fatuhat-i-Alamgiri," folio 74b.
14. "Brij Lal Pancholy," folio 161b.
15. Mustad Khan, p. 106.
16. "Jodhpur Rajya ki Khyat," 2:22.

the emperor granted an audience to the Jamrud officials and considered their request for recognition of the heirs of the late maharaja.[17] The Jamrud officers promoted the cause of Jaswant's scions largely out of self-interest. Imperial recognition of the infants and of the officers as protectors of the children would place the officers in positions of power and enable them to act as regents during the minority of Jaswant's heirs.

While Alamgir considered the petition of the Jamrud officials he also entertained rival claims for power in Jodhpur. Rani Hadi continued to advance her claim for imperial recognition,[18] as did Indra Singh, a grandson of Jaswant's disinherited elder brother and a Mughal mansabdar who had served Aurangzeb in the Deccan.

Aware of the growing factionalism in Marwar and of the dangers of a regency, Alamgir wisely tried to solve the succession dispute among the Rathors by retaining imperial control over Jaswant's sons. The emperor agreed to bestow suitable mansab and the gaddi of Marwar on Jaswant's heirs, provided the infants were brought up at the Mughal court.[19] He also tried to compensate the Jamrud officials for their reduced prospects by reconfirming their possession of the jagirs of Sojat and Jaitaran.[20] Both proposals were rejected; the Rathors argued that the infants could not be separated from their mothers, but they did promise that the children would attend the court at a later age.[21]

Alamgir grew increasingly suspicious of the motives of the Jamrud party. He felt that the rejection of his offer to raise the infant princes and to confer imperial appointments and royal titles on them indicated the greed and ambition of those who posed as the protectors of the children.

17. Ishwardas, folio 75a.
18. "Waqaya Sarkar Ajmer and Ranthambhor," p. 217.
19. Mustad Khan, p. 109.
20. "Brij Lal Pancholy," folio 174a.
21. Ishwardas, folio 75b.

Self-aggrandizement and personal gain, rather than concern over the stability of Marwar, seemed to be the main interests of the Jamrud officials. Alamgir accordingly attempted to resolve the succession dispute by recognizing Indra Singh Rathor as the ruler of Marwar on 26 May 1679.[22]

Alamgir selected Indra Singh to be raja of Jodhpur because he wanted a ruler who could stabilize the situation in Marwar. The death of Jaswant Singh seemed to provide the opportunity for a recrudescence of clan factionalism, and Alamgir wanted to avoid an internecine conflict within the Rathor clan. The emperor's selection for the gaddi of Marwar had distinguished himself as a mansabdar in the Deccan; as a result, he held the rank of commander of one thousand troops and had received an increase in his mansab as recently as June 1678.[23] More importantly, Indra Singh could legitimately claim the throne of Marwar since his grandfather, Amar Singh, was the disinherited older brother of Jaswant Singh.

Alamgir's appointment of Indra Singh signaled the start of conflict in Marwar; yet this battle for succession to the throne of Jodhpur was merely a continuation of the feud within the senior branch of the Rathor clan that had begun when Amar Singh refused to accept his father's selection of Jaswant as the ruler of Marwar. Amar had served the imperial court and was a recognized military commander, he had a quick temper that lost him his father's favor, imperial support, and the chance to live at the emperor's court.[24] Rai Singh, Amar's son, also served the Mughals. He perpetuated his father's hatred of Jaswant and, as explained above, was able for a brief period to oust Jaswant from the throne and gain appointment

22. Mustad Khan, p. 109.

23. See Archival Record no. 4988, Central Records Office, Hyderabad. The document is published in Yusaf Husain, *Selected Documents of Aurangzeb's Reign 1659–1706* (Hyderabad, India: Government of Andra Pradesh, 1958), p. 121.

24. Shah Nawaz Khan, *Maathir-ul-Umara*, 2:230–31, 236.

as raja of Marwar. Had Indra Singh courted the support of the Rathor nobility, he could have ended this long-standing feud and easily gained firm control of the Jodhpur throne, but because the new raja was backed by Mughal power he felt that he could exclude his kinsmen from power and defy the clan hierarchy just as Jaswant had. Indeed, Indra's attitude toward the Rathor nobility precipitated the conflict that Alamgir had hoped to avoid when he appointed Indra as raja of Marwar.

Shortly after the appointment of Indra Singh, the Jamrud Rathors decided to leave the imperial capital for Jodhpur. News of the reaction in Marwar to Indra Singh's nomination encouraged the Jamrud officials, who now hoped for a general uprising in favor of Jaswant's infant heirs. Alamgir anticipated the flight of the Jamrud party, however, and ordered that the infants be placed under the protective custody of the crown.[25] The arrival of imperial troops at the residence of the Jamrud Rathors precipitated their escape plans; and the death of one of the infants made a return to Jodhpur imperative, since the surviving heir of Jaswant could now serve as a single rallying point for a united Rathor resistance against Indra Singh and the Mughals. Under cover of darkness a contingent of the Jamrud party, dressed as common tradesmen, slipped by the Mughal guards, with the surviving infant, Ajit Singh, concealed in a vendor's basket.[26] When the Mughals finally discovered the Rathor ploy, they set out in hot pursuit of the refugees. The headstart that the Jamrud party gained from the ruse and a dilatory rearguard resistance that some of the Rathor troops offered against their pursuers enabled the officials to enter Marwar with the late maharaja's heir on 23 July 1679.[27]

Two members of the Jamrud party, Mukand Das Khichi

25. Iswardas, folio 75b.
26. "Waqaya Sarkar Ajmer and Ranthambhor," pp. 552–54.
27. Ishwardas, folio 110a.

and the wife of Thakur Mahkam Singh, conducted the infant
raja into Marwar.[28] The Rathor officials found refuge at Ba-
lunda, a village between Sojat and Jaitaran,[29] but since the
area was surrounded by Mughal strongholds the young Ajit
was transported to Kalindari in the district of Sirohi. At the
suggestion of Rani Devadiji, one of the widows of Jaswant
Singh, the child was entrusted to a local Brahman,[30] but this
arrangement was only temporary because, fearing Mughal
reprisals for harboring the fugitives, the Rao of Sirohi asked
the Jamrud party to leave his territory. The infant raja was
then taken to Nandolai, a village in Mewar.[31]

The Mughal presence in Marwar partially explains the secre-
tive and nomadic concealment of the infant Ajit, but an
equally important reason was the duplicity of Rathor clansmen. Both the Jamrud officials and the widowed ranis wanted
to prevent the Mughals from regaining possession of the infant, and they were similarly concerned that the young raja
would fall into the hands of a rival clique of the clan because
their jagirs and their property depended on their ability to
maintain control of the infant king. Continuity in the direct
male line of the senior branch of the clan would protect the
status quo, and the possibility of a regency under their aegis
offered the Jamrud officers increased opportunities for expanding their personal power.

Self-aggrandizement, rather than loyalty to the ruling house,
was the motive of the Jamrud officials. Whenever an opportunity occurred for improving their personal prospects,
whether in the services of Ajit Singh or of Indra Singh, a
Rathor Rajput would switch allegiance. For example, Champ-
avat Sonag and many other members of the Jamrud faction
defected to the side of the Mughal-appointed raja when he
offered them large increases in their jagirs, but when it became

28. "Waqaya Sarkar Ajmer and Ranthambhor," p. 554.
29. Ibid., p. 556.
30. "Ajit Granth," verse 331.
31. Ishwardas, folio 77a.

apparent that Indra Singh had no intention of fulfilling his promise to the Jamrud clique, they again supported Ajit Singh.[32]

Because each Rathor Rajput believed himself the equal of his raja, he felt no overarching loyalty to a particular clan leader. The clansmen who supported a ruler of Jodhpur usually did so for personal gain, and the strength of their commitment was dependent on their prospects for individual advancement. This peculiar parochialism coupled with the clandestine circumstances under which the infant Ajit entered Marwar prevented the development of any widespread Rathor reaction against Indra Singh and the Mughals.

One aspect of the escape from the imperial capital also worked to the disadvantage of the Jamrud party by creating a question about Ajit's legitimacy. To confuse the Mughals, the Jamrud officials had substituted the children of two slave girls for the royal infants. Alamgir adroitly proclaimed the slave children as the legitimate heirs of the maharaja and refused to acknowledge the successful escape of the Rathors.[33] The early seclusion of the refugees and the absence of the ranis from among the escapees added to the confusion of the incident.[34] The possibility existed that the Jamrud officials were merely trying to advance their own interests by posing as the protectors of an infant whose parentage was less than certain. It was because of these circumstances that the Jodhpur Rathors greeted the news of the escape of their Jamrud kinsmen with indifference and doubt.

To eliminate the suspicions surrounding their escape from Delhi and to rally waning support for their campaign against Indra Singh, the Jamrud officers, now under the leadership of Durga Das Rathor, decided to formally install Ajit Singh as

32. "Ajit Granth," verses 291–98.
33. Khafi Khan, 2:260.
34. The escaping Rathors decided to kill the ranis who had produced the posthumous sons of Jaswant Singh. The apparent motive for the murder of the queens was to prevent them from falling into Mughal hands.

ruler of Marwar on 2 August 1679.[35] There was no ground
swell of popular support for the infant raja, but some of the
Jamrud officials did succeed in mobilizing Rathor forces
against the Mughals. Sonag and Bhatti Ram, two of the
Rathors who had escaped from Delhi, reputedly ousted Ta-
hawar Khan, the military commander (*faujdar*) of Jodhpur,
from the Rathor capital; and Sujan Singh led a similarly
successful attack against the Mughals at Siwana.[36] Although
Rajput sources probably exaggerated the success of these
campaigns, in September 1679 the emperor dismissed Ta-
hawar Khan as faujdar and removed Indra Singh from the
gaddi of Marwar for their manifest inability to suppress disturbances, which indicates some success by the Rathors.[37]

It should be noted that at no time during the turbulent days
of August did the Jamrud officials make the presence of Ajit
Singh in the capital known. It is possible that the Rathors
ousted the Mughals from Jodhpur; if they did, even for a
brief period, one might expect a tumultuous salute to the
infant raja in the capital of Jodhpur. Instead, Durga Das and
his band of Rathor nobles harbored Jaswant's heir and continued to stay away from the capital until they finally found
shelter in the confines of the Aravallis.[38]

One reason for Durga Das's caution in concealing the
whereabouts of the infant raja was the overwhelming presence
of imperial troops in Marwar. The emperor arrived in Ajmer
on 25 September 1679 and assumed personal command of the
operations in the Rathor state.[39] He appointed many imperial
officials, including his son Prince Akbar, to pursue the Rathor
rebels. Alamgir also began preparations for the direct administration of Jodhpur by the crown.[40] He divided Jodhpur

35. "Waqaya Sarkar Ajmer and Ranthambhor," p. 332.
36. "Jodhpur Rajya ki Khyat," 2:52–53.
37. Mustad Khan, p. 110.
38. "Jodhpur Rajya ki Khyat," 2:44; Ishwardas, folio 77a.
39. Mustad Khan, p. 111.
40. Ibid., p. 112.

into districts and posted faujdars, thanadars, and other officers at appropriate points throughout the kingdom.

Critics of Alamgir usually interpret the emperor's campaign against Marwar and his absorption of the Jodhpur state into the imperial administration as an indication of his anti-Hindu sentiment.[41] In one sense, however, the emperor's actions can be seen as an effort to conciliate the Rathors of Marwar, since he did remove the unpopular Indra Singh from the throne of Jodhpur. Alamgir also appointed Rathors to imperial posts,[42] and many of Jaswant's civil administrators undoubtedly found employment in Mughal service. Alamgir's skill in gaining clan and civilian acceptance of Mughal rule partially explains the fact that the entire Rathor state was brought under the Mughal control by November. The only expression of Rathor discontent against Mughal rule occurred in the clan strongholds of Sojat and Jaitaran,[43] but a contingent of troops under the command of Hamid Khan easily crushed the resistance in these districts.

Alamgir's success in restoring order to Marwar through the pacification of the Rathor clan and the employment of civil administrators in the Mughal service illustrated the isolation of the Jamrud clique from the affairs of Marwar. The emperor's insistence that he, and not Durga Das, protected the real Ajit Singh continued to raise many doubts among the Rathor clansmen about the motives of the Jamrud faction.[44] Since members of the clan lineage felt no overriding loyalty to the heir of Jaswant Singh, Ajit's kinsmen increasingly cooperated with the Mughals and attempted to gain position or appointment in the imperial system.

Lacking support from the Rathors, the Jamrud officers, led by Durga Das, turned from Marwar and asked the Sisodias

41. Jadunath Sarkar, *History of Aurangzeb*, 3:325–29.
42. Mustad Khan, p. 112.
43. Ibid., p. 119.
44. Khafi Khan, p. 260.

of Mewar for assistance in their struggle against Alamgir. A new phase of the war opened when the ruler of Mewar, Raj Singh, agreed to protect the refugees.

chapter VII

Mewar and the Rathor Rebellion

Raj Singh, the Sisodian ruler of Mewar, viewed the succession struggle in Marwar with indifference. Rivalry and antagonism had always characterized the relations between the two leading houses of Rajwarra, and the death of Jaswant Singh at Jamrud probably evoked little sympathy among the ranks of the Sisodians. The Jamrud officials had formally notified Raj Singh of the demise of their leader,[1] but the reaction of the rana to the news of Jaswant's death is not known.

By contrast relations between the rana and Alamgir were quite cordial. Even the reimposition of the tax (*jaziya*) on all non-Muslims in the Mughal empire did not affect the friendship between the two rulers. Alamgir revived the tax that was levied primarily on the Hindus on 2 April 1679,[2] and later that month he issued a farman to Raj Singh assuring the rana of his continued support and friendship.[3] Alamgir also honored the rana's son, Jai Singh, at the imperial court and gave the young prince special gifts for his father in Udaipur, the Sisodian capital.[4]

Although the Sisodian ruler could look with disinterest at the clan factionalism within Marwar, he could not remain indifferent to the increasing number of Mughal forces in the Rathor state. The proximity of Mewar to Jodhpur and the formidable military strength of the Mughals in Rajwarra created an uneasiness in Udaipur. The emperor's decision to personally direct the operations against Marwar from Ajmer

1. "Brij Lal Pancholy," folio 153b.
2. Muhammad Hashim Khafi Khan, *Muntakhab-ul-Lubab*, 2:255.
3. The text of the farman appears in Kaviraja Shyamal Das, *Vir Vinod*, 2:457–59.
4. Saqi Mustad Khan, *Ma'asir-i-Alamgir*, p. 175.

created further apprehension in the Sisodian state. In late October 1679, the Sisodian ruler received a letter from the Jamrud nobles requesting his help in fighting the Mughals.[5] Much more than a military alliance hinged on the rana's acceptance of the Rathor proposal. Durga Das realized that Raj Singh's support was tantamount to a recognition of Ajit Singh as the legitimate heir of Jaswant Singh. The leader of the Jamrud faction hoped not only to enlist the support of Mewar against the Mughals, but also to unite the Rathors of Marwar by settling the question of Ajit Singh's legitimacy.

Rana Raj Singh faced a dangerous dilemma. He could not afford to ignore the huge Mughal military buildup in Marwar nor the presence of Alamgir at Ajmer. The emperor clearly intended to absorb Marwar into the imperial domains and, at the same time, to reduce the independence of Mewar. Harboring the Rathor refugees would signify open defiance of the imperial will and assure an invasion of Mewar by the Mughal forces. Raj Singh decided to play for time, possibly hoping for Rathor resistance to develop in Marwar. To the alternately solicitous and threatening letters of the emperor,[6] he submitted polite but evasive replies.[7] Finally, the Sisodian ruler agreed to protect the young Ajit from the Mughals and offered the infant prince and his party a jagir and military aid.[8]

It is not possible to give a precise explanation for Raj Singh's decision to support the Rathors. Since the rana assumed a position that was bound to provoke an imperial invasion of Mewar, he probably expected that his protection of the Jamrud party would precipitate a general uprising against the Mughals in Marwar and thereby divert the emperor's attention away from his own sedition. The early Rathor success in ousting the imperial faujdar from Jodhpur and the defeat of Indra Singh could have suggested to him that the Mughals were vulner-

5. "Jodhpur Rajya ki Khyat," 1:56.
6. Khafi Khan, p. 261.
7. Man Kavi, "Raj Vilas," canto 10, folios 137–40, verses 1–22.
8. Ibid., canto 9, folio 136, verses 200–206.

able, even though those events had occurred before Alamgir assumed direct control of the campaign in Marwar. It is also possible that the Sisodian nobility forced a decision upon the rana, since many clansmen supported the Jamrud party and had opposed the Mughals in Godwar, a district of Mewar, even before Raj Singh had opted to protect the Rathor refugees.[9] Another possibility is that Alamgir's policy, which offered the rana no alternatives but confrontation or a humiliating surrender to the emperor's demand for the return of the Rathors to imperial custody, could have precipitated Raj Singh's opposition to the Mughals.

In deciding to offer asylum to the Rathors and to defend the orphaned Ajit, Raj Singh probably recognized an opportunity to increase Sisodian prestige among the entire Rajput caste. Raj Singh had long been in the shadow of Jaswant Singh, but the Rathor's death at Jamrud had made the Sisodian the premier noble of the Rajputs. As guardian of the infant ruler of Marwar, Raj Singh could further enhance his power in Rajwarra by controlling the combined armies and prestige of the two leading Rajput states.

Raj Singh's strategy against the Mughals apparently was to maximize the natural defenses of Mewar. He posted garrisons at critical points in the rugged defiles of the Aravalli Range hoping to trap Mughal forces in their approach to Mewar. The rana personally assumed responsibility for the defense of Deobari Pass,[10] a narrow gateway to Udaipur that bisected a spur of the Aravallis about fifteen miles east of the Sisodian capital.

Alamgir left Ajmer for Mewar on 30 November 1679.[11] Before leaving the provincial capital, he dispatched advance forces to secure Mandal, a city in the northern plain of Mewar. He also ordered his eldest son, Prince Muazzam, to approach the rana's territory from his post in the Deccan and Muham-

9. Ishwardas, "Fatuhat-i-Alamgiri," folio 77b.
10. Man Kavi, canto 10, folio 146, verse 78.
11. Mustad Khan, p. 180.

mad Amir Khan, subahdar of Ahmadabad, to attack Mewar from the southwest. In this way, Mughal forces completely surrounded Mewar and eliminated any possibility of a retreat.

The Mughals' successful capture of Mandal and their penetration into Mewar through the Aravallis alarmed the Sisodias. The arrival of Alamgir at Mandal in mid-December and the appearance of another son, Prince Azam, with additional forces from Bengal raised further alarm in Udaipur. To meet the crisis, Raj Singh decided to evacuate the capital city and to remove the royal family to the confines of the hills of Bhomat, south of Udaipur.[12]

By the end of December 1679, Alamgir had advanced from Mandal to the approach of the Deobari Pass. On 4 January 1680, he attacked the Sisodian forces defending the pass and won an overwhelming victory.[13] The emperor immediately dispatched a force to capture Raj Singh in Udaipur, but the imperial troops found the rana's capital abandoned and desolate.[14] Two weeks later, however, the Mughals stumbled onto the Sisodian camp in the hills of Bhomat and inflicted heavy damage on the rana's troops and supplies.

Alamgir remained in Mewar for two months. During that period he consolidated imperial control over the rana's territory and destroyed any materiel that might be of use to the rebels. He established strong Mughal garrisons in Udaipur and Chitor and appointed his favorite son, Prince Akbar, as administrator of Mewar with a force of twelve thousand troops. At the end of February the emperor prepared to leave Mewar for Ajmer, where he arrived on 22 March 1680.[15]

Aurangzeb's brief campaign in Mewar broke the spirit of the Rajputs. The emperor had humiliated Raj Singh by his easy victory over the Sisodian forces at Deobari, and the

12. Das, 2:465.
13. Mustad Khan, p. 186.
14. Khafi Khan, 2:263.
15. Mustad Khan, p. 190.

imperial occupation of the royal capital embarrassed the rana further. Alamgir's military success reduced the proud Sisodian ruler to the status of a refugee in his own territory and shattered the alliance between the Rathors and the Sisodians. Only evasive tactics by Raj Singh prevented the imperial forces from capturing the fugitive Rajputs, who ultimately found shelter in the rugged ridges of the Aravallis that separated Marwar from Mewar.

Durga Das and his Rathor followers once again were forced to flee from the pursuit of the Mughals, but this time in territory that was largely unfamiliar to them. Finally, they managed to evade Mughal patrols and return to Marwar, where they created local agitation against the Mughals in the traditional Rathor strongholds of Sojat and Jaitaran.[16] Alamgir, piqued at the Rathors' success in evading Mughal troops, issued a farman on 7 April 1680 that directed an imperial force to pursue the rebels.[17] Indra Singh, the former raja of Jodhpur, was also deputed by Alamgir to search for his rebel kinsmen. In May, Indra Singh and Durga Das met at the battle of Khetsasr,[18] from which Durga Das and his Jamrud faction emerged victorious. When the news of Durga's victory spread throughout Marwar, it prompted many local uprisings against the Mughals.[19] Indra Singh, after his defeat, tried to bolster his own chances of regaining the throne of Jodhpur by bribing Durga Das, but the rebel leader refused to be bought.[20] Durga Das was so exuberant about his victory over Indra Singh that that he contemplated an attack on the Rathor capital, but a strong Mughal force in Jodhpur dissuaded him from such a rash action.[21]

The deteriorating situation in Marwar prompted Alamgir

16. "Jodhpur Rajya ki Khyat," 2:57.
17. "Akhabarat-i-Darbar," year 12, p. 129, Bikaner Collection.
18. Vir Bhan, *Raj Rupak*, pp. 58–60, verses 21–39.
19. Mustad Khan, p. 121.
20. "Ajit Granth," verses 470–74.
21. Ibid., verses 481–85.

to recall Prince Akbar from Chitor. The emperor delegated the young prince the responsibility for the pacification of southern Marwar and ordered him to secure Sojat against Rathor attack and to pursue the rebels into their strongholds in the Aravallis. Prince Akbar arrived in Marwar in mid-July 1680. He camped at Sojat where he decided to establish his base of operations.[22] After nearly three months of searching for the rebels, he encountered the main force of the Rathors at Nadol, a village southwest of Sojat. On 11 October 1680, Prince Akbar and the Mughal forces inflicted such heavy losses on the Rathors that the rebels sued for an immediate peace.[23]

Even before the defeat at Nadol, the rebels had submitted a peace proposal to the emperor. Khafi Khan relates that Durga Das and Rana Raj Singh had approached Prince Muazzam about a peace settlement; but the prince's suspicions of the proposal and interference in the negotiations by Nawab Bai, the prince's mother, rendered the proposals fruitless.[24] There is no indication that a military defeat prompted these earlier peace proposals by the rebels. Alamgir had succeeded, however, in splitting the Rathor forces in September 1680 by granting a jagir to Rani Hadi,[25] the widow of Jaswant, who had remained one of the leaders of the Jodhpur opposition to Mughal rule. These divisions within the forces of his Rathor allies may have been what convinced Raj Singh to enter into negotiations with the Mughals.

The defection of Rani Hadi from the Rathor cause and the defeat of the rebel forces at the battle of Nadol struck a mortal blow to the hopes of Durga Das for recovering the throne of Jodhpur for the young Ajit Singh. The death of Rana Raj Singh on 22 October 1680 added a further note of

22. Mustad Khan, p. 119.
23. Ishwardas, folios 77a, 78b.
24. Khafi Khan, 2:300.
25. "Akhabarat-i-Darbar," year 12, pp. 239–40, Bikaner Collection.

pessimism to the Rathor rebellion against Mughal authority. Because of the division in the ranks of his kinsmen and the confusion in the camp of his Sisodian ally, Durga Das embarked on a desperate course of pillage and plunder in the Mughal-held territory of Marwar.[26]

After Prince Akbar's victory at Nadol, Alamgir ordered his son to pursue the rebels into the Aravallis. Akbar planned to enter the mountains through the Deosuri Pass, one of the narrow trans-mountain passages from Marwar into Mewar. Anticipating the Mughal strategy, Rana Jai Singh, the eldest son of Raj Singh and the successor to his deceased father as ruler of Mewar, ordered his younger brother Bhim to oppose the Mughal advance.[27] Akbar penetrated the Aravallis and met the Sisodian forces at Jhilwara, a large village ten miles south of the Deosuri Pass. Once again the Mughal army overwhelmed its Rajput opponents. On 22 November 1680, Akbar gained control of Jhilwara and routed the Sisodian forces.

Meanwhile, Durga Das's campaign to rally Rathor support against the Mughals had failed miserably. His attacks on the villages controlled by Alamgir's men amounted to little more than banditry,[28] and his raids earned him the animosity of the people of Marwar. When the news of the battle of Jhilwara reached Durga Das, the Rathor leader decided to submit to Mughal authority. The fact that Durga Das did not mention the gaddi of Marwar when he surrendered to the emperor indicates the desperate plight of the Rathor party. The Jamrud officials, after challenging Mughal control for more than a year, retreated from their early demand that the throne of

26. "Waqaya Sarkar Ajmer and Ranthambhor," p. 605.

27. Man Kavi, canto 10, folio 146, verse 14.

28. Durga Das had kidnapped two merchants of Sojat who had cooperated with the Mughals and then released them after receiving a ransom. Such acts reduced the prestige of the rebel leader and dissipated any remaining support for his cause among the war-weary people of Marwar. An account of Durga's pillage in Marwar appears in "Waqaya Sarkar Ajmer and Ranthambhor," pp. 605–6.

Marwar be given to Jaswant's heir and merely petitioned that
a small jagir be granted for the support of the infant Ajit.[29]
Alamgir, recognizing the weakness of the Rathor's position,
refused to consider their proposal.

The triumph of the imperial armies in Marwar and in Mewar reduced the importance of the Rajput rebellion in the
mind of the emperor. The emperor was preoccupied with the
opportunities for Mughal expansion in the Deccan that followed the death of the Maratha leader Shivaji in early April
1680 and felt that the sorry circumstances of the Rathor rebels
no longer merited imperial attention. Rajput affairs were
again thrust into the imperial consciousness, however, when
Prince Akbar, supported by both the Rathors and the Sisodias, declared himself emperor at Nadol on 3 January 1681.[30]

29. Ibid., p. 545.
30. "Ajit Granth," verse 537.

CHAPTER VIII

THE IMPERIAL PHASE OF THE RAJPUT REBELLION: PRINCE AKBAR'S REVOLT

Akbar's military success at Nadol and Jhalwara sparked an ambition in the young prince to challenge his father on the battlefield and to depose Alamgir by defeating him in combat, just as Aurangzeb had deposed Shah Jahan. The promise of Rajput support fanned Akbar's ambition: Durga Das intimated that all of Marwar would rise in rebellion once Akbar took the field against his father, and Raj Singh of Mewar promised to place his resources at the disposal of Akbar in the contest for the Mughal throne.[1]

Prince Akbar declared himself emperor at Nadol on 3 January 1681. Had the young prince immediately coordinated his forces for an attack on his father at Ajmer, he could have easily won the Mughal throne because Alamgir had dismissed his commanders after his apparent victory over the Rajputs and was nearly defenseless. Instead of pressing the attack, however, Akbar dallied for two weeks while preparing his troops for the clash with Alamgir. In the interim, the emperor regrouped the imperial forces at Ajmer and welcomed the returning armies of Shahabuddin Khan, Hamid Khan, and Prince Azam.[2]

Akbar's delay in attacking his father's army and the news of the returning Mughal forces caused dismay among the ranks of the Rajputs who had already tasted defeat at the hands of Alamgir. Finally, Akbar took the field against his

---

1. Details of the agreement between Akbar and the Rajputs are contained in a letter from the rebel prince to Shambhuji, the Maratha leader. The letter is found in "Khatut-i-Shivaji," folio 19.

2. Saqi Mustad Khan, *Ma'asir-i-Alamgir*, p. 198 .

father on 22 January 1681, nearly three weeks after he had proclaimed himself emperor.

Meanwhile, Alamgir had not really accepted his son's rebellion. In an attempt to avoid the impending battle with the rebel prince, the emperor asked Inayat Khan, the new faujdar of Jodhpur, to summon Inayat's son-in-law, Tahavvur Khan, to the imperial camp.[3] Tahavvur Khan was Prince Akbar's first lieutenant and had arranged the alliance with the Rajputs. Alamgir knew that Akbar accepted Tahavvur's counsel and hoped that by convincing the khan of the futility of a rebellion, a confrontation might be avoided. On entering the imperial tent, however, Tahavvur Khan refused to disarm in accordance with Mughal custom. The Mughal nobility took offense at the arrogance of the khan and baited him with insults. The rebel noble responded by unsheathing his sword and was immediately cut down by Alamgir's officers.[4]

The emperor still wanted to avoid a conflict with his favorite son, so he devised a plan by which he hoped to destroy the Rajput support for Prince Akbar. Tahavvur Khan's death merely increased the likelihood of the plan's success. Shortly after his nobles had killed Akbar's lieutenant, Alamgir wrote a letter to the rebel prince congratulating him on his alliance with the Rajputs.[5] The emperor suggested that Akbar's rebellion had merely been a ruse to ensnare the Rajputs in a pitched battle against the Mughals, and he urged Akbar to place the Rajputs in a battlefield position between the Mughal forces. Alamgir then caused the letter to fall into the hands of Durga Das. When the Rathor leader tried to obtain an explanation of the letter from Akbar, he was told that the prince was sleeping and was refused admission to the prince's quarters. Durga Das then approached the tent of Tahavvur Khan, but he could not locate Akbar's commander. The Rathor Rajput interpreted the inaccessibility of Akbar and the ab-

---

3. Muhammad Hashim Khafi Khan, *Muntakhab-ul-Lubab*, 2:274–75.
4. Ibid., p. 275.
5. Mustad Khan, p. 201.

sence of Tahavvur Khan as part of an imperial conspiracy and immediately ordered his troops to abandon Akbar's camp.[6]

When the rebel prince awoke on 26 January 1681, the day designated for the battle with Alamgir, he found his camp deserted and his baggage plundered.[7] The departing Rajputs had ravaged Akbar's supplies and captured his treasury, leaving him without troops or funds. Alamgir's plan had succeeded beyond expectation. The hapless prince began to despair, but the return of Durga Das prevented him from submitting to his father's authority. The Rathor leader had found out about Alamgir's ploy and had decided to return to Akbar's camp. There was no chance of giving battle to Alamgir, however, because the combined forces of Akbar and Durga Das totaled only about four hundred men.[8]

The small size of the rebel force commanded by Durga Das was a result of the limited appeal of the cause of Ajit Singh among the Rathor clansmen. The Jamrud officials had tried in vain to enlist the support of their kinsmen in Jodhpur, but Mughal control over the Rathor kingdom and the question of Ajit's legitimacy as well as the traditional clan factionalism prevented any large-scale support from developing in Marwar. The support of Raj Singh of Mewar had temporarily increased their numbers, but the rana's death in November 1680 augured a further diminution in the prospects of the Jamrud faction because Jai Singh, the new rana of Mewar, had never supported the Rathor cause with the enthusiasm of his father. Durga Das's success in convincing Prince Akbar to rebel against his father proved to be only a temporary respite from the frustration that had characterized the Rathor's attempt to gain support in his battle against Alamgir. The young prince was no match for his father on the battlefield or in diplomacy; his indecision and his inability to inspire confidence in his troops created dissension among his followers even before the fateful

6. Ishwardas, "Fatuhat-i-Alamgir," folio 83a.
7. Mustad Khan, pp. 123–24.
8. Khafi Khan, 2:275.

events of January 25 and 26. Although Durga Das succeeded
in getting the rebel Akbar to recognize Ajit Singh as the legitimate heir of Jaswant Singh,[9] the title of maharaja and the
mansab as commander of seven thousand troops that ac-
companied the recognition were worthless unless Akbar gained
the Mughal throne. When Alamgir tricked the Rajputs into
deserting Akbar he also nullified any advantage that the
Jamrud officials had gained from Akbar's recognition of Ajit
by formally decreeing that the infant who was in imperial
custody was the legitimate son and heir of Jaswant Singh.[10]

The cumulative effect of their military and diplomatic defeats at the hands of the emperor was catastrophic for the
Jamrud officials; they were isolated from their clansmen and
deprived of Rajput and imperial allies. Nonetheless, Durga
Das, once again joined with Akbar, decided to make one last
attempt to foment a large-scale rebellion against imperial
authority. The first task facing Akbar and Durga Das was to
escape from the pursuing forces of Alamgir, which were
under the command of the emperor's son, Prince Muazzam.[11]
Muazzam encountered the fugitives near Sanchor, a town
fifteen miles southwest of Jalore.[12] He reportedly proposed to
grant the gaddi of Jodhpur to Ajit Singh and the subah of
Gujerat to Akbar,[13] but such a proposal seems unlikely given
the precarious resources of the rebels. It is more likely that
Muazzam offered a jagir to Durga Das for the return of the
rebel Akbar,[14] but the Rathor leader apparently held out
for a more lucrative offer because his party proceeded from
Sanchor to Mewar. In Mewar, the rebels soon recognized the
futility of soliciting support from Rana Jai Singh because,
shortly after his desertion from Akbar's camp, the Sisodian

9. "Akhabarat-i-Darbar," year 24, pp. 10–11, Bikaner Collection.
10. Mustad Khan, p. 127.
11. Ishwardas, folio 83b.
12. Mustad Khan, p. 126.
13. "Jodhpur Rajya ki Khyat," 2:63.
14. Vir Bhan, *Raj Rapuk*, p. 167, verse 239.

ruler had proposed peace to the Mughals.[15] Durga Das's request for additional support apparently occurred in the midst of the negotiations with Alamgir (March–April 1681), and the rana refused to jeopardize his position by granting asylum or support to the fugitives from Mughal rule. Rebuffed in his attempt to resurrect the Rajput alliance against Alamgir, Durga Das decided to approach the Maratha leader, Shambhuji, with a similar proposal directed against the Mughal emperor.

The formal negotiations between Jai Singh of Mewar and Alamgir's representative, Prince Azam, resulted in a peace settlement known as the Treaty of Rajsamudra. Ratified on 24 June 1681, the accord provided for the cession of the village clusters (*paraganas*) of Mandal, Pur, and Badnor to the empire in lieu of the payment of jaziya.[16] The Mughals agreed to restore all other territories to the rana and to withdraw all of their forces stationed in the Sisodian state. Alamgir also agreed to grant official recognition to Jai Singh as the ruler of Mewar and to confer on the rana the mansab of commander of five thousand troops.[17]

The terms of the treaty were extremely advantageous for Mewar. The rana salvaged Sisodian prestige from his defeat by the Mughals and managed to emerge with his title intact and with most of his ancestral lands, except for those paraganas that were ceded to the Mughals in lieu of jaziya. There were several reasons why Alamgir made a settlement so favorable to Mewar. First, the emperor had lost interest in the affairs of Rajwarra. The death of Shivaji in 1680 had shifted his attention to the Deccan, and he had become absorbed in ex-

15. A farman from Alamgir to the rana dated 23 February 1681 suggest that negotiations had taken place shortly after the events of 25–26 January 1681. The farman appears in Kaviraja Shyamal Das, *Vir Vinod*, 2:651–52.

16. Chapter 10 discusses jaziya and its effect on Mughal-Rajput relations.

17. Mustad Khan, pp. 207–8.

panding Mughal influence in the south. Secondly, Alamgir did
not consider Jai Singh a threat to Mughal rule. The young
raja had challenged imperial authority and had paid a terrible
price for his actions. By conferring a suitable mansab on the
rana and by confirming his succession to the gaddi of Mewar,
Alamgir implemented the same policy of conciliation toward
the Rajputs that the Mughals had used since the reign of
Emperor Akbar. A final reason for Alamgir's generous treatment of Mewar was the emperor's intention of securing his
northern flank before embarking on his campaign in the
Deccan. Alamgir probably thought that a favorable settlement for Mewar would enable him to call on the rana for troop
support during his operations in the south.[18]

The Treaty of Rajsamudra signaled the end of the Rajput
rebellion against Alamgir. The two great houses of Rajwarra,
the Sisodias of Mewar and the Rathors of Marwar, were no
longer allies against imperial authority. Mention has already
been made of Jai Singh's refusal to aid Durga Das and Prince
Akbar in their flight from Alamgir. The rana of Mewar not
only failed to offer support to the Jamrud party but he actually
sent his brother, Bhim Singh, to Ajmer to help the Mughals
govern Marwar.[19]

After the signing of the Treaty of Rajsamudra, the isolation of Durga Das and his followers from both their Rathor
kinsmen and their Sisodian allies was complete. The officials
who had served the late Jaswant Singh at Jamrud could claim
to protect his legitimate heir, but they could not pretend to
represent the interests of the Rathor clan or of the Jodhpur
state. Each of the many setbacks they had encountered had
reduced the number of Rathors who followed Durga Das's
leadership and lessened their chances of defying Mughal rule.
Even though they had joined forces with Akbar, Akbar's entire
entourage at the time that he and Durga Das fled to the

18. Amar Singh, Jai Singh's successor, did in fact supply a contingent
of troops to Alamgir for the campaign in the Deccan. See Das, 2:746.
19. Ishwardas, folios 83b, 84a.

Deccan consisted of only three hundred men, most of whom were the prince's original followers.[20] The number of Rajputs was even smaller because many Rathors had deserted Durga Das and returned to Marwar. After the failure of Akbar's rebellion, most of the Rathors and the civil administrators in Jodhpur decided to accept imperial rule and attempted to obtain positions in the Mughal administration of the state. Even Durga Das reportedly petitioned the emperor for an imperial appointment, but Alamgir denied his request.[21]

The Jamrud Rathors and Durga Das still claimed to act in the interests of Ajit Singh, the heir of Jaswant Singh; but Ajit's cause was really their own because only in the triumph of the maharaja's heir could they find positions of power and prestige. Rejected by the Rathors, the Sisodias, and the Mughals, their only hope for success was to gain the support of the Maratha leader, Shambhuji, who was also at war with Alamgir.

Durga Das and Prince Akbar arrived in Maratha territory on 11 June 1681.[22] Shambhuji granted them asylum and provided for their maintenance,[23] but his initial reaction to the arrival of the rebels was cool. The Maratha leader was suspicious of Durga Das and Prince Akbar because he feared an alliance between them and his younger brother, Raja Ram. When Akbar tried to increase his army by recruiting mercenaries, Shambhuji informed him that his forces had to remain the same size as when the rebel prince first entered Maratha territory.[24]

The relationship between Akbar and Shambhuji improved somewhat after a personal meeting in November 1681, but the Maratha leader was more concerned with defending his territory against Alamgir than with aiding Akbar and Durga

20. Khafi Khan, 2:275.
21. "Waqaya Sarkar Ajmer and Ranthambhor," p. 545.
22. Mustad Khan, p. 202.
23. Ibid., p. 211.
24. "Akhabarat-i-Darbar," year 24, 16 August 1681, Royal Asiatic Society Collection.

Das. The emperor had left Ajmer for the Deccan on 8 September 1681 and proceeded to advance toward the Maratha kingdom,[25] and his presence in the south prevented Shambhuji from giving the rebel prince any substantive support. For the next five years, Akbar and Durga Das beseeched the Maratha leader for aid, but their requests went unanswered.[26] Finally, disillusioned by the evasive and ambiguous replies of the Maratha ruler, Akbar decided to seek support for his cause from another quarter. In February 1687,[27] the Mughal prince set sail for the court of Shah Abbas, the king of Persia. Durga Das, equally disappointed at the duplicity of Shambhuji, left the Maratha kingdom and returned to Marwar in August 1687.[28]

25. Ishwardas, folio 84a.
26. Samples of the correspondence from Akbar and Durga Das to Shambhuji appear in Jadunath Sarkar, *The House of Shivaji*, pp. 201–11.
27. Khafi Khan, 2:279.
28. "Ajit Granth," verse 1428.

CHAPTER IX

THE AFTERMATH OF THE REBELLION: MEWAR AND MARWAR

The Treaty of Rajsamudra proved to be the basis of a lasting peace between the Sisodian Rajputs and the Mughals. Jai Singh concentrated on restoring prosperity to his kingdom, which had suffered greatly during the brief war with Alamgir. The Sisodian ruler repaired public works and encouraged agricultural recovery. In 1691 he opened Jai Samudra, an artificial lake to be used for irrigating the central plain of Mewar.

Alamgir apparently appreciated Jai Singh's pledge of cooperation with the empire. The Mughal ruler honored the Sisodian Rajput with valuable gifts shortly after they had signed the Treaty of Rajsamudra.[1] The emperor further honored Jai Singh by conferring the title of raja on his younger brother, Bhim Singh, and by posting Bhim Singh at Ajmer as a mansabdar in the imperial service.[2]

The cordial relations between Mewar and the empire continued under Jai Singh's successor, Rana Amar Singh, who ruled from 1698 to 1707. Alamgir recognized Amar Singh as the legitimate heir of Jai Singh and confirmed his title to the traditional Sisodian territories. Amar Singh responded to the emperor's actions by sending a contingent of Sisodian Rajputs into imperial service in the Deccan.[3]

The situation was quite different in Marwar, where recalcitrant Rathor clansmen continued to offer resistance to Mughal rule. Sonag Bhatti, a Rathor who had been one of Jaswant Singh's officers at Jamrud, attacked imperial forces in the area around Jaitaran; and similar attacks by Rathors occurred

1. Muhammad Hadi Kanwar Khan, "Tarikh-i-Chaghatai," 2:128.
2. Ishwardas, "Fatuhat-i-Alamgiri," folio 84a.
3. Kaviraja Shyamal Das, Vir Vinod, 2:746.

at Didwana and Makrana.[4] However, when the Rathors directly challenged the Mughals in pitched battle, the result was usually a victory for the imperial forces. In November 1681 at Merta, for example, more than five hundred Rathors fell to the Mughal army commanded by Itiqad Khan.[5] The only record of a major Rathor victory from 1681 to 1687 was the battle of Khanana in which the Rajputs captured the town of Siwana and killed the fort commander (*qiladar*), Purdil Khan.[6]

Although all of these Rathor uprisings had only local impact and were of fleeting military consequence, they were symptomatic of the prevalent discontent with Mughal rule in Marwar. The Rathor Rajputs had ruled the Jodhpur state for two centuries, and the transition from the quasi independence of a vassal state to the regimentation of direct Mughal rule was quite difficult. This change from kingdom to khalsa was undoubtedly responsible for the undercurrent of resentment and resistance that existed throughout Marwar, but more substantive reasons than Rathor pride can be found to explain the attacks on the Mughals from 1681 to 1687.

First of all, a resurgence of clan authority occurred in the years immediately after Jaswant Singh's death. The maharaja had so skillfully isolated the clan lineage from the exercise of power in Marwar that his death was a signal for every clansman to assert himself. Jaswant's apparent failure to produce a male heir guaranteed the appearance of civil strife throughout Marwar; Ishwardas's famous observation that each household in the kingdom prepared to create mischief after the maharaja's death was an accurate assessment of the mood of Marwar at that time.[7] Indra Singh and the Mughal officials who administered the Jodhpur state were the authority figures against whom this resentment of centralized political power

4. "Akhabarat-i-Darbar," year 24, 13 July (for a description of the attack on Jaitaran), 13 November (for Didwana), 16 November (for Makrana) 1681, Royal Asiatic Society Collection.

5. Ishwardas, folio 85a.

6. Saqi Mustad Khan, *Ma'asir-i-Alamgir*, p. 166.

7. Ishwardas, folio 74b.

was directed. The Rathor clansmen wanted positions of power consistent with their self-esteem, and they were prepared to challenge any Rajput or Mughal who attempted to perpetuate the state of subjection that Jaswant had reduced them to.

This desire for self-assertion permeated all segments of the clan lineage. The most outstanding example of it during the period of adjustment to Mughal rule (1681–1687) was the battle of Khanana. The Rajputs who defeated the Mughals and gained control of the fort of Siwana were Kumpawats, members of a subclan of the Rathors who had been relegated to positions of minor importance during the reign of Jaswant Singh.[8]

A second factor that accounted for the continued Rathor antagonism toward the Mughals was the frustration felt by many of the Jamrud officials and administrators who had supported Ajit Singh. Durga Das had won the loyalties of many of these Rathors by promising them lucrative offices and appointments on the accession of the infant Ajit to power. Durga Das's failure to win imperial recognition for Ajit and his flight to the Deccan after continual defeats by the Mughals added to the disappointment of the Rathors who had supported the Jamrud party for the sake of future rewards. Excluded from imperial service because of their support for Durga Das and deprived of royal appointment by the failure of the Rajput rebellion, many Rathors resorted to pointless banditry and plunder to improve their personal situations. Sonag Bhatti, for example, had alternately supported Ajit Singh and Indra Singh without any personal gain and, when he realized that Indra Singh's promises were as fruitless as those of Durgas Das, he attempted to challenge Mughal authority for his own profit.[9]

Indian historians such as Jadunath Sarkar and other, more recent historians such as V. S. Bhargava and S. R. Sharma in-

8. "Jodhpur Rajya ki Khyat," 2:72–73.
9. "Akhabarat-i-Darbar," year 24, 13 July 1681, Royal Asiatic Society Collection.

terpret these spasmodic attacks on the Mughals as an expression of clan sentiment for the heir of Jaswant Singh and
as evidence of a people's war in his support.[10] The Rathors of
Marwar, however, felt little loyalty for Ajit Singh. Their in-
termittent challenges to Mughal authority merely reflected
clan frustration over the centralization of political power in
Jodhpur. Clansmen desired to regain the prerogatives they
had lost during the reign of Jaswant Singh and had been un-
able to recover at Jaswant's death because of the installation
of Indra Singh as raja and the subsequent imposition of direct
imperial control over Marwar.

The number of Rathors who supported Ajit Singh declined
precipitously after the Treaty of Rajsamudra. The defeat of
the combined Rathor and Sisodian forces and the failure of
Prince Akbar's rebellion illustrated the futility of opposing
the Mughals. Dissension appeared among the ranks of Ajit's
adherents, and even the Jamrud officials who were Ajit's most
loyal allies began to question the wisdom of prolonging the
conflict with the Mughals. Some Rathors resented Durga
Das's retreat to the Deccan while others took offense at the
confinement of the young Ajit Singh under the protection of
Durga's lieutenant, Mukand Das Khichi, and the rebel leader's
kinsman from Bilara, Bhagwan Das.[11]

The divisions among the Jamrud faction of the Rathors
developed into open antagonism when Durga Das discovered
on returning to Marwar in August 1687 that, contrary to his
orders and over the objections of Mukand Das Khichi, some
of the Rathor nobles had removed Ajit Singh from his confinement five months earlier.[12] Durga Das immediately realized
that his position as guardian of Jaswant's heir was being chal-

10. Jadunath Sarkar, *History of Aurangzeb*, 3:245–49; V. S. Bhargava,
Marwar and the Mughal Emperors, p. 136; S. R. Sharma, *Mughal Empire in India*, p. 408.
11. "Jodhpur Rajva ki Khyat," 2:77–78.
12. Ibid., 2:79.

lenged by his kinsmen. Accordingly, he did not proceed to Ajit's headquarters after he entered Marwar.[13]

When the news of Durga Das's return to Rathor territory reached Ajit's court, the young raja, then in his eighth year, delighted at the prospect of meeting his protector. Of the Rathor nobles who resided with Jaswant's heir, however, only Hada Durjan Sal shared Ajit's enthusiasm for the return of Durga Das.[14] Durjan Sal informed Durga Das of the situation at Ajit's court and decided to join the Rathor rebel.[15]

Young Ajit sent for Durga Das, but the Rathor noble refused to attend the prince's court. Disregarding the suggestions of his advisers, the impatient youth decided to go himself to see his former protector. When Durga Das learned of the boy's approach, he advanced to meet him and cast himself at Ajit's feet.[16] The young prince became enamored of the Rathor warrior and decided to join Durga Das in his campaign against the Mughals. Shortly after their reunion, Durga Das led an attack on an imperial garrison at Sojat. The Mughals repulsed the Rathors and inflicted heavy casualties on them. Durga Das fled the battlefield and barely escaped his Mughal pursuers.[17] The grim realities of warfare jolted the young prince, who had approached battle with the Mughals as if it were a boyhood adventure. Ajit became disillusioned with Durga Das and rejoined the other Jamrud officials, who urged a reconciliation with the Mughals.

Changes in the imperial administration of Marwar favored a rapprochement with the Mughals. Alamgir had appointed Shujaat Khan, the subahdar of Gujerat and a gifted administrator skilled in the command of troops, to supervise the operations in Marwar. The khan analyzed the situation in

13. "Ajit Granth," verses 1510–13.
14. Ibid., verses 1501–9.
15. Ishwardas, folio 121a.
16. "Ajit Granth," verses 1527–32.
17. Ibid., verses 1548–55.

Marwar and acted accordingly: he dispatched troops to pursue
Durga Das, and at the same time he cultivated a friendship
with Ajit Singh.[18] The new military commander realized that
much of the turmoil in Marwar was caused by the frustration
of the Rathor nobles and of the civil administrators, and he attempted to remedy this situation by giving many of the disgruntled Rathors positions in the administration of the state.[19]
Shujaat Khan's policy of reconciliation attracted many of
Durga Das's followers and strengthened the position of the
peace-seeking Rathors who surrounded Ajit Singh. In 1690 the
khan, through the faujdar of Ajmer, offered Ajit a jagir and
mansab.[20] Ajit proceeded to Ajmer against the advice of Durga
Das, who had learned of the Mughal offer; but the Rathor
prince later fled the provincial capital when news reached him
that imperial forces had captured his headquarters at Siwana.[21]

These events changed the attitudes of both Durga Das and
Ajit Singh toward the Mughals. When he learned of the defeat of Ajit Singh's forces at Siwana, Durga Das recognized the
futility of further resistance to imperial rule and, after having
battled the emperor's armies for more than ten years, he decided to cooperate with the Mughals. Conversely, Ajit Singh,
who had entered into negotiations with the Mughals, resented
the duplicity of the Ajmer proposal and vowed revenge for the
seizure of Siwana. The young prince gathered the Rathor
forces that remained loyal to him and prepared to attack
Mughal positions in Marwar.

In dealing with Durga Das and Ajit Singh, Shujaat Khan
continued his dual policy of incentive and intimidation. He
appointed Rathors and civil administrators to imperial posts.
One of his most significant nominations was the appointment
of Ishwardas Nagore to the office of revenue agent (*amin*) of

18. "Akhabarat-i-Darbar," year 24, 7 April 1688, Royal Asiatic Society Collection.
    19. Ali Muhammad Khan, *Mirat-i-Ahmadi*, 1:326.
    20. Vir Bhan, *Raj Rupak*, pp. 326–28, verses 28–37.
    21. "Jodhpur Rajya ki Khyat," 2:90–91.

Jodhpur in 1695. The author of "Fatuhat-i-Alamgiri" was subsequently instrumental in obtaining imperial pardon for Durga Das. At the same time that Shujaat Khan courted Rathor nobles, he also took steps against the Rathor rebels by sending his son, Muhammad Qasim, to fight Ajit Singh. In May 1695 Shujaat's son inflicted heavy losses on the armies of the rebel prince.[22]

Depressed by his repeated defeats at the hands of Shujaat Khan and by his inability to rally his war-weary forces, Ajit Singh petitioned the emperor for the grant of a jagir and mansab. In 1699 Alamgir responded by conferring on Ajit a jagir of Jalor, Sanchor, and Siwana. He also appointed the young Rathor commander of fifteen hundred troops in the imperial service.[23] In the following years, Ajit, in an attempt to increase his mansab, asked the emperor for permission to attend the imperial court. Alamgir replied by immediately giving the sum of three thousand rupees to Ajit and also promising to provide an additional jagir to the Rathor prince upon his arrival at the court.[24] The heir of Jaswant Singh continued to serve Alamgir as an imperial mansabdar until the emperor's death in 1707.

Durga Das also entered imperial service. Disillusioned with the unappreciative Ajit Singh, the aging Rathor warrior decided to abandon his former ward and to pursue his fortune in the service of the Mughals. Because Durga Das held in his custody the son and daughter of Prince Akbar, he was able to ask Ishwardas, the amin of Jodhpur, to obtain for him an imperial pardon and a suitable jagir in exchange for the return of the emperor's grandchildren. In May 1698 Durga Das took the Mughal princess, Saif-un-Nisa Begam, to her grandfather's court, where he received mansab and jagir from the emperor.[25] The Mughal ruler later increased Durga Das's rank

22. "Akhabarat-i-Darbar," year 38, 27 May 1695, Royal Asiatic Society Collection.
23. Ibid., year 43, 2 December 1699.
24. Ibid., year 44, 16 November 1700.
25. Ishwardas, folios 167a, 167b.

and his jagir in exchange for Akbar's son, Prince Buland Akhatar.[26] Alamgir apparently accepted Durga Das's pledge of loyalty to the empire because in 1699 he employed the Rathor noble on the very delicate mission of meeting his former ally Prince Akbar, who reportedly planned to reenter Mughal territory from his retreat in Persia.[27] Durga Das went to Qandhar in Afghanistan to escort the prince to the imperial court, but the report of Akbar's return to India proved to be a baseless rumor. Durga Das left Qandhar for the Deccan, where he was subsequently made a faujdar of Patan, a town in Gujerat.[28]

The appointments of Ajit Singh and Durga Das to the imperial service ended the Rathor rebellion against Alamgir. The participation of the Rathor leaders in the service of the emperor whom they had fought for twenty years illustrates the precise nature of the revolt against Alamgir. The rebellion was not a general uprising by the people of Marwar against Mughal authority nor a concerted effort by the Rathor clan to resist Mughal imperialism; it was merely a contest between competing factions of the Rathor clan for control of the offices and revenues of Marwar. Alamgir initially permitted the Rathors to compete against each other, but when the conflict threatened to develop into an interminable civil war, he intervened.

The disinherited Jamrud faction continued to offer resistance to Alamgir long after the issue of succession in Marwar had been settled because, as the protectors of Jaswant Singh's heir, they would lose the most through the incorporation of Jodhpur into the Mughal empire. Durga Das and the Rathor nobles who had served Jaswant Singh at Jamrud refused to accept the limited prospects that Mughal control of Marwar offered them; consequently, they tried unsuccessfully to rally clan support against Alamgir, to enlist Sisodian aid in defense of Rajwarra, to divide Mughal power by encouraging the

26. Muhammad Khan, 1:323–33.
27. Mustad Khan, p. 412.
28. Muhammad Khan, 1:348.

revolt of Prince Akbar, and, lastly, to recruit Maratha forces to help in their fight against Aurangzeb. Each of these setbacks reduced the ranks of the Jamrud nobles and eventually converted the cause of Ajit Singh to a vendetta between Durga Das and Alamgir. The emperor, however, faced problems in the Deccan that dwarfed his concern over the fate of the rebel Durga Das. Finally, the dissension between Durga Das and Ajit Singh returned the rebellion to its original status as an internal feud between competing interests of the Rathor clan. During Alamgir's lifetime, the rebel leader and the Rathor prince could salvage only minor imperial appointments for their twenty-year struggle against Mughal rule.

CHAPTER X

RELIGION AS A FACTOR
IN THE RAJPUT REBELLION

Modern historians generally consider the Rajput rebellion against Alamgir as a Hindu-Muslim confrontation.[1] They view the alliance between the Rathors of Marwar and the Sisodias of Mewar as evidence of widespread discontent among the Hindu subjects of the Mughal empire, and they see Alamgir's revival of the jaziya as the catalyst that caused a deeply rooted Hindu resentment to find expression in open rebellion against Mughal authority. Although such an interpretation establishes thematic continuity between the seventeenth-century Rajput rebellion and the communal tensions of the twentieth century, it is not consistent with the facts of the revolt against Alamgir.

Certain developments during the course of the Rajput rebellion suggest the inaccuracy of interpreting the conflict as a Hindu-Muslim confrontation. Alamgir's appointment of Indra Singh to the gaddi of Marwar and the raja's continued support of Alamgir after the emperor assumed direct control over Marwar are two aspects of the revolt that are difficult to understand if one accepts the communal explanation of the rebellion.[2] Similarly, the Rajput support for Prince Akbar seems to belie the idea of a Hindu-Muslim conflict.[3] The acceptance of an imperial mansab by Bhim Singh, the younger brother of Rana Jai Singh of Mewar, and his subsequent duty in Marwar against his former Hindu allies also seem to be incompatible with the notion of the rebellion as a religious conflict.[4]

1. A. L. Srivastava, *The History of India,* p. 649; S. R. Sharma, *Mughal Empire in India,* pp. 398–409.
2. Saqi Mustad Khan, *Ma'asir-i-Alamgir,* p. 109; Ali Muhammed Khan, *Mirat-i-Ahmadi,* 1:326.
3. Jadunath Sarkar, *A History of Aurangzeb,* 3:356.
4. Ishwardas, "Fatuhat-i-Alamgiri," folio 84a.

Much of the controversy that surrounds the Rajput rebellion centers on Alamgir himself. The emperor's attempt to establish Islamic orthodoxy at the imperial court has led many historians to suggest that Alamgir's campaign against the Rajputs was part of an imperial design to convert all of India to the religion of Muhammad. Critics of Alamgir find evidence of the emperor's religious bias in the imperial farmans that Aurangzeb issued shortly after gaining control of the Mughal throne. In a decree issued from Benares in February 1659, Alamgir prohibited the building of new Hindu temples and the repairing of old ones.[5] A series of rigid regulations aimed at establishing puritanical restrictions at the imperial court followed the promulgation of the Benares farman: the emperor banned music and dancing, prohibited gambling and alcohol, eliminated public parties and festivals, and imposed imperial standards of dress and appearance.[6]

A condemnation of Alamgir based on these measures ignores the complexity of the emperor's religious policies. Even though the Benares farman prohibited construction or repair of Hindu temples, it also prohibited the Mughal officials in Benares from interfering with or disturbing the Brahmans or any other Hindus who visited the temples.[7] Neither can the court regulations that Alamgir sponsored properly be considered anti-Hindu in tone because many of the ordinances affected Muslims as well. The prohibition against music, for example, also applied to religious hymns sung on the anniversary of the birth of the Prophet.

Although iconoclasm has been seen as the underlying motive for all of Alamgir's actions, many enactments sponsored by the emperor actually had no religious relevance at all. One such measure was the discontinuance of the darshan, a Mughal custom introduced by Akbar of appearing on a

5. Jadunath Sarkar, *A Short History of Aurangzeb, 1618–1707*, p. 147.
6. S. R. Sharma, *The Religious Policies of the Mughal Emperors*, pp. 111–15.
7. Sarkar, *A History of Aurangzeb*, 3:281.

palace balcony to acknowledge crowds assembled outside the imperial grounds. Jadunath Sarkar believes that Alamgir eliminated the darshan because of its similarity to the Hindu practice of saluting one's tutelary idol at the beginning of each day.[8] A more practical reason for its elimination, however, was that it was inconvenient and dangerous. As Pringle Kennedy points out, "If the emperor did not appear at the fixed hours, stories of his death got about."[9] Because Shah Jahan failed to observe darshan in September 1657, rumors of his death precipitated the war of succession among the emperor's four sons. It was for this reason that Alamgir decided to discontinue the custom of darshan.

Perhaps the most universally condemned measure that Aurangzeb enacted was the jaziya. Because this tax applied only to non-Muslims, it is always cited by critics of Alamgir as evidence of the emperor's anti-Hindu bias. To this single piece of legislation is ascribed the alienation of the Rajputs, Sikhs, Satnamis, Marathas, and all the other non-Muslim communities that raised their voices in protest against Mughal rule. Jaziya has been damned as the "original sin" of Alamgir that haunted later Mughals.[10] It has also been labeled an obnoxious tax that finally and completely alienated all Hindus from the empire and thereby resulted in the overthrow of the monarchy.[11]

The effect of the jaziya on Mughal-Rajput relations is not clear. The timing of Alamgir's reenactment of the tax has led some historians to consider the measure as the impetus for a final call to arms by the Rajput race against the bigotry of the Muslim emperor. S. M. Edwards and H. L. G. Garrett, for example, view the alliance between Raj Singh of Mewar and Durga Das of Marwar as a national uprising in Rajputana

8. Sarkar, *A Short History of Aurangzeb*, p. 103.
9. Pringle Kennedy, *A History of the Great Moghuls*, p. 89.
10. Ram Sharma, *The Making of Modern India*, p. 169.
11. James Tod, *Annals and Antiquities of Rajputana*, p. 462.

in defense of country and religion.[12] But the belief that Alamgir's passage of jaziya precipitated the alliance between the Rajputs of Mewar and Marwar ignores the earlier indifference of Raj Singh to the fate of the Rathors. As noted in Chapter 6, the Sisodian ruler of Mewar did not become alarmed at the threat that the Mughals posed to his state until Alamgir amassed larged imperial forces at Ajmer in preparation for the direct administration of Marwar.

The interpretation that the Rathor-Sisodian alliance reveals Mewar's support for a Hindu rebellion against the emperor overlooks the fact that relations between Raj Singh and Alamgir remained cordial even after the enactment of jaziya and that his son Jai Singh was a guest at the imperial court until the end of April 1679. At the time that the prince returned to Mewar, carrying with him a farman and several presents from Alamgir for his father, there was no evidence of animosity between Mewar and the empire.[13] Furthermore, there is no record of Raj Singh protesting against the reinstitution of jaziya. As G. N. Sharma notes, "Had there been any such protest, the local annalists who have given minute details of other events would not have left this unnoticed."[14]

The only indication of a formal protest against jaziya is a curious letter of unknown authorship. Three copies of the letter exist: one in the Royal Asiatic Society in London, a second in the possession of the Asiatic Society of Bengal in Calcutta, and a final copy in the confidential papers of the maharana of Udaipur. The letter condemns Alamgir's reimposition of the jaziya as inconsistent with the established Mughal policy of religious toleration and states that the tax levied on the Hindus was inexpedient and bound to result in the eventual disgrace of the name and honor of the Timurid

12. S. M. Edwards and H. L. G. Garrett, *Mughal Rule in India,* p. 84.

13. Mustad Khan, p. 175. The text of Alamgir's letters to Raj Singh appears in Kaviraja Shyamal Das, *Vir Vinod,* 2:457–59.

14. G. N. Sharma, *Mewar and the Mughal Emperors,* p. 144.

dynasty.[15] At one time Jaswant Singh was thought to be the
author of this note. Orme, in his *Historical Fragments,* attrib-
utes the letter to the maharaja of Jodhpur,[16] but subsequent
research has shown that Jaswant Singh died before the reimposition of jaziya. James Tod and Kaviraja Shyamal Das, on
the other hand, ascribe the protest to Rana Raj Singh.[17]
Sarkar asserts that the style and content of the letter suggest
that only Shivaji could have written it,[18] but a later Indian
historian has challenged Sarkar's hypothesis and claims that
the author was Raj Singh.[19]

In spite of the debate about the authorship of the letter,
all of the above-mentioned historians agree that the note
represents a general Hindu protest against Alamgir's religious
intolerance. Recent research has suggested, however, that the
traditional accounts of Alamgir's iconoclasm are not completely in accord with historical evidence. B. N. Goswamy and
J. S. Grewal, for example, have published a document that
shows that Alamgir was guaranteeing Hindu rights in the
Punjab at the same time that he was conducting his campaign
against the Rajputs.[20] Similar evidence introduced by Janan
Chandra shows that Alamgir's attitude toward his Hindu
subjects is much more complex than was once thought.[21]

Alamgir's policy toward the Rajputs was not an anti-Hindu
crusade against the traditional warrior caste, but a campaign
of limited objectives aimed at expanding Mughal influence

15. "Khatut-i-Shivaji," folio 13.
16. Robert Orme, *Historical Fragments of the Mughal Empire, of
the Morattoes, and of the English Concerns in Indostan,* p. 87, note 49.
17. Tod, 1:442, note 2; Das, 2:462.
18. Jadunath Sarkar, "Letters of Shivaji."
19. Yashpal, "Origins of the Rajput War 1679–81."
20. See Document 9 in B. N. Goswamy and J. S. Grewal, *The
Mughals and the Jogis of Jakhbar,* pp. 125–39.
21. Janan Chandra, "Alamgir's Attitude Towards Non-Muslim In-
stitutions," *Journal of Pakistan Historical Society,* no. 7 (1957), pp.
36–39; "Alamgir's Tolerance in the Light of Contemporary Jain Literature," *Journal of the Pakistan Historical Society,* no. 6 (1958), pp.
269–72.

in Rajwarra. His appointment of Indra Singh as successor to Maharaja Jaswant Singh indicates that his initial intention was to preserve the identity of the Jodhpur state. However, the inability of Indra Singh to maintain order in his kingdom and the continued disturbances created by the Jodhpur faction of the Rathor clan convinced Alamgir to resolve the conflict by absorbing Marwar into the imperial domain.

Alamgir's decision to assume direct control over Marwar alarmed Raj Singh, who felt that protecting the Jamrud Rathors from the Mughals would give him an opportunity to increase his bargaining power with Alamgir and a chance to increase his prestige in Rajwarra. The rana's refusal to surrender the refugees to imperial officials is what precipitated the year-long conflict between the Sisodias and the Mughals.

Interpreting the alliance between the Sisodias of Mewar and the Jamrud Rathors as a Hindu alliance against the Muslim emperor distorts the motives of both the rebels and Alamgir. The contest between the Rajputs and the Mughals was not a communal confrontation but a struggle between a parochial, traditional political system and an expansionist empire. The Rajputs fought in defense of their clan-dominated political structure, not in defense of their religion. The later participation of the Sisodian ruler in the Mughal service and the appointment of the rebel Rathor leaders to imperial posts indicates the precise nature of the conflict and the inadequacy of interpreting the encounter through a religious perspective.

CHAPTER XI

CONCLUSION

The Rajput rebellion against Alamgir started as a succession dispute in Marwar and developed into a conflict that threatened the stability of the Mughal empire. Although this challenge to Mughal authority was only a limited confrontation and not a general uprising by the Rajput clans, the alliance between the leading houses of Rajwarra and the coalition between the Rajput rebels and Prince Akbar nearly cost Alamgir his throne.

Alamgir was able to take advantage of the peculiar sociopolitical system of the Rajputs to prevent the rebellion from developing into a prolonged conflict. The clan structure of the Rajputs consisted of branches (*shakhas*) and septs that each promoted its individual interests. As long as the chances of military success seemed high, the clan could maintain a united front and control the individual aspirations of its members. The threat of failure, however, or even a temporary setback in fortunes, would precipitate a breakup of the fissiparous elements within the clan organization. As a result, the Rajputs were incapable of making the long-term commitment that a challenge to Mughal authority required.

The physiographic configurations of Rajwarra also contributed immensely to the limited outlook of the Rajput clan. The Aravalli mountains bifurcated Rajwarra, and the rugged defiles of the range offered even the minor chieftains a place in which they could assert their sovereignty. From the security of their mountain fortresses, the clan leaders were able to defy stronger adversaries and resist the incursions of larger political systems. This natural fragmentation promoted a parochial political mentality and permitted a proliferation of princely states in Rajwarra.

Egalitarianism within the clan hierarchy was an equally important cause of the parochial outlook of the Rajput states. Each kinsman considered himself the equal of his clan leader, since all members of the clan structure traced their lineage to a common ancestor. No individual could assert himself in the clan hierarchy without first establishing support groups and securing alliances with his kinsmen; to gain political power and leadership it was necessary to establish an equilibrium of interests within the clan membership. The raja thus presided over a sociopolitical organization composed of distinct branches and septs each of which considered itself the equal of the ruling family.

In Marwar, Jaswant Singh used Mughal power to attempt to break the control of the Rathor clan over the gaddi. By participating in the mansabdari system, Jaswant constructed a base of power that was independent of the clan hierarchy. His prestige as an imperial officer and his power as a military commander in the Mughal service precluded any challenge to his authority by his kinsmen. Supported by the threat of Mughal intervention in the event of a clan uprising, Jaswant fashioned an administrative structure that revolutionized the traditional power equation between the raja and the nobility in Marwar. Patterning his organization after the system used by the Mughals Jaswant appointed Brahmans and merchants as well as non-Rathor Rajputs to state offices and, breaking with Rathor tradition, excluded his kinsmen from a share of the political power in Marwar.

The introduction of Mughal military power as an element in the Rajput polity testified to the success of the Timurids as rulers of the subcontinent. Through matrimonial alliances and imperial honors, the Mughals had penetrated Rajwarra and converted the Rajputs' cautiousness toward their rule into competition for their favor. The ultimate expression of Mughal control in the princely states was the right to decide the line of succession; conferral of the right to rule (*tika*) by the Mughal emperor certified a candidate's competency and legitimized his rule in the eyes of the empire. Although the Mughals usually accepted the nominee of the clan or of the raja, occasionally the emperor exercised imperial prerogative and arbitrarily selected a candidate in order to avoid a succession dispute.

Alamgir's policy in Marwar following the death of Jaswant Singh at Jamrud in Afghanistan provides an interesting example of imperial intervention in a Rajput state. Alamgir appreciated the Rathors' desire to determine their clan leader, but he was also aware of the potential for civil war that existed in the Jodhpur state. The Rathor noblity, who had grudgingly accepted Jaswant's centralization of power, greeted the maharaja's death with a resolve to reassert clan authority over the gaddi of Marwar. Jaswant's failure to produce a male heir facilitated a resurgence of clan rights, but the absence of an authority figure against whom the nobles could direct their protest plunged the kingdom into chaos and disorder. In May 1679, after five months of internecine warfare among the Rathors, Alamgir decided to settle the succession dispute by appointing Indra Singh as raja of Marwar.

Although Indra Singh possessed a legitimate claim to the gaddi of Marwar, the Rathor nobility refused to accept his appointment. Because of Indra's past association with the Mughals they suspected that the new raja would use imperial support against them, just as Jaswant had. Some Rathors decided to promote the cause of Ajit Singh, the late maharaja's son, born two months after his father's death. The clan hierarchy in Marwar soon realized, however, that the opportunities that would result from a regency would be monopolized by the Jamrud faction of Rathor nobles who held custody of the maharaja's infant son. Since the Rathor clansmen felt little loyalty toward Jaswant's heir they began to cooperate with the Mughals in an attempt to gain positions and appointments in the Mughal administration of Jodhpur.

Alamgir had imposed imperial control over Marwar in order to prevent the continuation of clan disturbances, but Indra

Singh proved incapable of ending the civil strife. Because Jodhpur was economically and strategically significant for the stability of Rajwarra, the emperor could not permit the situation to deteriorate any further, so he assumed personal control over the affairs of the state. Alamgir also realized that imperial control ot Marwar would present him with additional opportunities for the assignment of jagirs to the Mughal nobility. By the second decade of Alamgir's reign, the land available for such appointments (*paibaqi*) was quite limited. The emperor's disastrous policy of frontier expansion, while failing to produce any additional territory, had swelled the ranks of the imperial nobility and caused a backlog of paper promotions and unfulfilled promises. Extension of imperial rule into Marwar would give the emperor an opportunity to meet some of these obligations.

Alamgir's absorption of Marwar into the imperial domain and lack of support from their Rathor kinsmen forced the Jamrud Rathors, now under the leadership of Durga Das, to find shelter outside of the Jodhpur state. Raj Singh, the ruler of Mewar, had long been in the shadow of Jaswant Singh, and he welcomed the opportunity to increase his prestige in Rajwarra by harboring the infant heir of the late maharaja. The flight of the Jamrud officials into Mewar widened the dimensions of the Rathor challenge to Mughal authority. Initially, the conflict had been only a succession dispute in Marwar, but Raj Singh's decision to grant asylum to the Rathor refugees broadened the uprising into a Rajput rebellion against the Mughals.

Alamgir recognized the significance of the alliance between the Jamrud Rathors and the Sisodias, and he resolved to crush the rebellion before all of the princely states of Rajwarra entered into the conflict. Mughal forces descended on Mewar from Gujerat, the Deccan, and Marwar. Within three weeks imperial troops occupied Udaipur, the Sisodian capital, and forced Raj Singh and the Jamrud Rathors into an ignominious retreat.

Raj Singh's death in November 1680 struck a mortal blow to the prospects of the rebel Rajputs; without the leadership and prestige of the rana, they had little hope of success. In a desperate attempt to salvage some concessions from Alamgir the rebels convinced his son, Prince Akbar, to declare himself emperor in January 1681. Even with the addition of a royal prince to their ranks, however, the Rajputs were no match for Alamgir. Alamgir used both stratagem and force to defeat the coalition of rebels and finally split their forces by signing a separate treaty with Jai Singh, the new ruler of Mewar.

The Treaty of Rajsamudra between Alamgir and Jai Singh ended the Rajput rebellion. The emperor recognized the new rana as the legitimate ruler of Mewar and granted him imperial rank and appointment. Alamgir's generous treatment of Mewar belies the suggestion by modern critics that the Rajput rebellion was the product of the emperor's bigotry. Had Alamgir resolved to crush the Hindu Rajputs, he could easily have done so. Instead, the emperor accorded Jai Singh imperial status and accepted the rana's pledge of support. Mewar remained at peace with the empire for the next thirty years, and Jai Singh even provided troops to Alamgir for his campaigns in the Deccan.

Alamgir's defeat of the Rajput forces eliminated any possibility of clan support in Marwar for the Jamrud faction and convinced the Rathor nobility that continued resistance to Mughal authority was fruitless. Completely isolated from his kinsmen in Marwar, Durga Das sought shelter with Prince Akbar at the court of the Maratha leader, Shambhuji. With Alamgir close by in Mewar, Shambhuji was fearful for the fate of his own kingdom and refused to commit any troops to Akbar's cause or to permit the rebel prince to recruit an army within Maratha territory. Akbar and Durga Das remained in Maharashtra for five years. Finally, in 1687, the rebel prince decided to avoid his father's wrath by escaping to Persia. Deprived of his imperial ally and rebuffed in his attempt to strike an alliance with the Marathas, Durga Das returned to Marwar.

Even in Jodhpur, however, the Rathor rebel was ignored by his kinsmen and rebuffed by the young Ajit, who had become disillusioned with the struggle against the Mughals.

A settlement with the recalcitrant Durga Das and the young Ajit Singh could then be made at the emperor's convenience. Both the aging warrior and the boy prince indicated a willingness to accept imperial appointment, and Alamgir eventually granted an imperial office to each of them. The Rajput rebellion, which had started as a challenge to Mughal authority, ended with the recognition that the emperor, not the clan hierarchy or the Rathor ruler, ultimately determined the affairs of Jodhpur. Alamgir had absorbed Marwar into the imperial domains in 1680, and the once proud Rathor state remained an integral part of the Mughal empire for the rest of his reign.

Alamgir's policies toward Rajwarra during the period of the Rajput rebellion indicate that he was aware of the distinctive features of the major princely states. In Marwar, the emperor recognized Jaswant Singh's success in reducing the traditional control by the clan hierarchy of the throne. Aurangzeb also realized that the chaos and disorder in the Rathor state following Jaswant's death were more than a succession dispute among the various factions of the clan membership, that they reflected the clan's attempt to regain privileges that had been lost during Jaswant Singh's reign. After the emperor's futile attempt to resolve the dispute by the appointment of a Rathor clansman to the Jodhpur throne failed, he brought Marwar under direct Mughal control because he realized that no policy other than outright annexation could stabilize the situation in Marwar.

In contrast to the succession dispute in Jodhpur, the accession of Jai Singh to the throne of Mewar after the death of his father, Raj Singh, occurred without incident. Because there was no threat of civil war in Mewar, Alamgir recognized the new ruler of the Sisodian state and granted him imperial rank, even though the emperor could have easily absorbed the occupied Mewar into the imperial domains as he had Marwar.

In attempting to establish thematic continuity between communal tensions in the twentieth century and the Mughal-Rajput confrontation of the seventeenth century, modern historians have overlooked the complexity of Alamgir's policy in the Rajput rebellion. Critics of Alamgir have dealt in facile generalizations and ignored the dynamics within the Rajput clan-state and the intricacies of an imperial policy designed to meet specific conditions in Rajwarra.

Alamgir always approached the Rajput states with an imperial perspective. The emperor could not permit civil war in Marwar to disrupt the stability of the entire region, nor could he overlook the opportunity to increase Mughal influence in the affairs of Mewar. In each case, however, local conditions determined imperial decisions. Alamgir's ability to isolate the Jamrud faction from their Rathor kinsmen and his skill in defeating the Sisodian rana and in detaching Mewar from the alliance with Prince Akbar testify to the success of his policies in Rajwarra.

GLOSSARY

The designation (P) or (R) after the entries indicates Persian and Rajasthani words respectively.

amir (P)	امير	noble
bakshi (P)	بخشى	paymaster
dastak (P)	دستک	pass permit
diwan (P)	ديوان	treasurer
farman (P)	فرمان	emperor's order
faujdar (P)	فوجدار	military commander
gaddi (R)	गद्दी	throne
jagir (P)	جاگير	territorial revenue grant
jagirdar (P)	جاگيردار	holder of a jagir
jaziya (P)	جزيه	Muslim tax on infidels
khalsa (P)	خالصه	imperial territory
khyat (R)	ख्यात	historical chronicle
kos (R)	कोस	a measure of distance varying from one-half mile to two and one-half miles.
kotwal (P)	كوتوال	magistrate
kshatriya (R)	क्षत्रिय	warrior caste
lodi (R)	लोदी	junior wife
mansab (P)	منصب	imperial appointment determining rank and status in Mughal administration

97

mansabdar (P)	منصبدار	holder of an imperial appointment
mantri pravan (R)	मनत्री प्रवन	prime minister in Mewar
nawis (P)	نویس	writer
paibaqi (P)	پایباقی	land available for jagir appointments
pargana (P)	پرگنه	cluster of villages
patrani (R)	पटरानी	mother of the heir apparent
pradhan (R)	प्रधान	prime minister
qiladar (P)	قلعدار	fort commander
rana (R)	राना	raja of Mewar
rani (R)	रानी	queen
sarkar (P)	سرکار	territorial administrative region
shakhas (R)	शाखा	clan branches
shudra (R)	शूद्रा	peasant
subah (P)	صوبه	province
subahdar (P)	صوبهدار	governor of a province
thanadar (P)	تهانادار	garrison commander
tika (R)	तिका	right to rule
vadi (R)	वदी	first wife
vakil (P)	وکیل	agent or ambassador
vanshavali (R)	वंशावली	genealogy
waqaya (P)	وقایع	events
waqaya-i- (P) nawis	وقایعنویس	writer of events, reporter

Bibliography

Primary Sources

Unpublished Manuscripts

Persian

"Akhabarat-i-Darbar." London. Royal Asiatic Society; Bikaner, India. Rajasthan State Archives. The "Akhabarat" were the official daily records of the affairs transacted at the imperial court.

"Fatiyah-i-Ibriyah." By Shihab-ud-Talish. London. British Museum. Persian Manuscript Collection, Add. 25, 422. Talish was one of Mir Jumla's aides and a participant in the campaigns in Kooch Behar and Assam.

"Fatuhat-i-Alamgiri." By Ishwardas. London. British Museum. Persian Manuscript Collection, Add. 23, 884. Ishwardas was a Hindu who held imperial appointment under Aurangzeb. He served as an official in Jodhpur for six years and enjoyed the confidence of the Rathors and the Mughals. His text is an extremely valuable and objective contemporary account of Aurangzeb's reign.

"Insha-i-Haft Anjuman." By Udiraj Tala-Yar. Transcript. Calcutta. Indian National Library. Jadunath Sarkar Collection. The author of this work was the son of the secretary of Jai Singh, the raja of Amber. The text is actually a compilation of the letters between Jai Singh and Alamgir, which were found in Benares by Jadunath Sarkar.

"Khatut-i-Shivaji." London. Royal Asiatic Society. Persian Manuscript Collection. This work is a compilation of the letters, farmans, and other documents that passed between the Mughals and the Marathas during the reign of Aurangzeb.

"Shah Jahanama." By Inayat Khan. London. British Museum. Persian Manuscript Collection, Oriental 175. Inayat Khan worked as Keeper of the Imperial Library under Shah Jahan. He was a close friend of the emperor and his history surveys the reign of his patron from 1627 to 1654.

"Tarikh-i-Aurangzeb." By Abul Fazl Mamuri. This work is a

general history of Aurangzeb's reign from his victory in the war of succession in 1657 to his death in 1707. Mamuri at one time served as recorder of events (*Waqaya-i-nawis*) in the employment of Aurangzeb's brother, Murad, but he subsequently accepted an appointment with Alamgir around 1660. Mamuri's attendance at the imperial court for the first two decades of Alamgir's rule makes the text a particularly valuable source for the first half of the emperor's reign.

"Tarikh-i-Chaghatai." By Muhammad Hadi Kanwar Khan. 2 vols. Udaipur, India. Saraswati Bhandar Library. The author of this history of Mughal rule was an imperial servant of Emperor Bahadur Shah (1707–1712). Although not a contemporary work of the Rajput rebellion, it is based primarily on official sources that the author had at his disposal.

"Waqaya-i-Ajmer, 1678–80." Transcript. Aligarh, Madhya Pradesh, India. Aligarh Muslim University. Department of History Research Library. By the seventeenth century, the Mughal emperors had posted an agent or writer (*nawis*) to the major Rajput courts. The main task of the nawis was to inform the emperor of any princely decisions or events (*waqaya*) affecting imperial interests. The reports of these agents are known collectively as waqaya-i-nawis.

"Waqaya Sarkar Ajmer and Ranthambhor." Hyderabad, India. Asafiya Library. This undated and anonymous manuscript is believed to be a contemporary source for the Rajput rebellion. The author, probably a newswriter (*waqaya-i-nawis*) in the employ of the Mughals, apparently held positions at Ajmer and Ranthambhor and finally with the imperial army in the Rajput war. The manuscript is invaluable as a first-hand account of the conflict and of the events that led to the dispute.

Rajasthani

"Ajit Granth." Jodhpur, India. Pustak Prakash Library. This anonymous eighteenth-century Rajasthani poem traces the lineage of Ajit Singh and the Rathor struggle against Alamgir.

"Brij Lal Pancholy." Transcript. Sitamau, India. Raghuvir Singh Library. This anonymous manuscript is a contemporary source for the Rajput rebellion. The author seems to have been a minor official in the service of Jaswant Singh.

"Haqiqat Bahi." Bikaner, India. Rajasthan State Archives. Jodhpur Records Section. These administrative reports for Marwar date back to the early eighteenth century.

"Jodhpur Rajya ki Khyat." 4 vols. Transcript. Sitamau, India. Dr. Raghuvir Singh personal library. The "Khyat" is the Rajasthani prose chronicle patterned on the Mughal court histories. This particular work is a history of the Rathor clan of Marwar. Although apparently compiled under royal patronage, the exact author is unknown.

"Kharita Basta." Bikaner, India. Rajasthan State Archives. Jodhpur Records Section. These files preserve the correspondence between the maharaja of Jodhpur and his kinsmen. They also contain some letters from the princes of Rajwarra to the ruler of Marwar. None of the documents is earlier than the eighteenth century, however.

Sanskrit

"Raj Ratnakar." By Sada Shiva. Udaipur, India. Saraswati Bhandar Library; Transcript. London. Royal Asiatic Society. Tod Manuscript Collection. This seventeenth-century Sanskrit poem is a general history of Mewar. The author served as an official under Raj Singh.

Published Works

Persian

Abdul Hamid Lahori. *Badshahnama*. Edited by Kabir al-Din Ahmad and Abd al-Rahim. Vol. 2. Calcutta: Royal Asiatic Society of Bengal, 1867. This work is the official history of the first twenty years of Shah Jahan's reign.

Abdul Qadir Badauni. *Muntakhab-al-Tawarikh*. Edited by Ahmad Ali. 2 vols. Calcutta: Royal Asiatic Society of Bengal, 1848. Written in the last years of the sixteenth century, this work is a general survey of the history of India from the Ghaznavides (c. 1000 A.D.) to Akbar's fortieth regnal year (1596).

Abu Fazl-i-Allami. *Ain-i-Akbari*. Translated by H. S. Jarrett and edited by Jadunath Sarkar. 2 vol., 2d ed. Calcutta: Royal Asiatic Society of Bengal, 1949. Abu Fazl was the official court historian of Emperor Akbar. His chronicle is an authoritative contemporary survey of Mughal history from the founding of the dynasty under Babur to the forty-sixth year of Akbar's reign (1602).

Ali Muhammad Khan. *Mirat-i-Ahmadi*. Edited by Syed Nawab Ali. 2 vols. Baroda: Gaekwad Oriental Series, 1927–1928.

Ali Muhammad Khan was the last Mughal diwan of Gujerat. Written in the late eighteenth century, his history is a valuable account of Gujerat as a province of the Mughal empire.

Aqil Khan Razi. *Waqiat-i-Alamgiri*. Edited by Khan Bahadur Maulvi Hafi Zafar Hasan. Delhi: Mercentile Press, 1946. This is a contemporary account of the contest for the Mughal throne among the sons of Shah Jahan. It provides a valuable description of Jaswant's activities during the succession struggle. Aqil Khan Razi apparently was a Mughal official who had access to many of the imperial documents.

Jahangir. *Tuzuk-i-Jahangiri*. Translated by Alexander Rogers and edited by Henry Beveridge. 2d ed. Delhi: Munshiram, 1968. Emperor Jahangir (1569–1627) is the author of this court history.

Mirza Muhammad Kazim. *Alamgirnama*. Edited by Khadim Husain and Abd al-Hai. Calcutta: Royal Asiatic Society of Bengal, 1868. The *Alamgirnama* was the official court history for the first ten years of Aurangzeb's reign.

Muhammad Hashim Khafi Khan. *Muntakhab-ul-Lubab*. 2 vols. Edited by Maulavi Kabir al-Din Ahmad and Ghulam Qadir. Calcutta: Royal Asiatic Society of Bengal, 1869. This work is a general history of the Mughals that emphasizes the reign of Aurangzeb. Khafi Khan was a court official during Alamgir's rule, and he witnessed many of the major events of the late seventeenth century. Originally published in 1734, the text presents a very detailed objective account of Aurangzeb's entire reign.

Muhammad Salih Kambu. *Amal-i-Salih*. Edited by Ghulam Yazdani. Vol. 3. Calcutta: Royal Asiatic Society of Bengal, 1939. This text is a contemporary seventeenth-century history of Shah Jahan.

Saqi Mustad Khan. *Ma'asir-i-Alamgiri*. Edited by Agha Ahmad Ali. Calcutta: Royal Asiatic Society of Bengal, 1870–1873. Saqi Mustad Khan was an imperial mansabdar under Aurangzeb. At the request of Inayat Khan, Alamgir's favorite secretary, Saqi Mustad Khan wrote his history of Aurangzeb shortly after the emperor's death in 1707.

Shah Nawaz Khan. *Maathir-ul-Umara*. Translated by H. Beveridge and B. Prasad. 3 vols. Calcutta: Royal Asiatic Society of Bengal, 1941. This text is an authoritative biographical dictionary of the Mughal nobility from the time of Babur to the eighteenth century.

Rajasthani

Bankidas. *Bankidas ki Khyat.* Jaipur: Rajasthan Oriental Research
    Institute, 1956. Bankidas was the court poet and historian
    of the Rathor ruler, Man Singh. Written in the early nine-
    teenth century, the text is a compilation of more than two
    thousand short notes on the history and culture of Marwar.
    The original manuscript is in the Anup Singh Library of the
    Maharaja of Bikaner.
Mahinot Nensi. *Khyat.* 4 vols. Jodhpur: Rajasthan Oriental Re-
    search Institute, 1960. This seventeenth-century prose chron-
    icle is an invaluable source for the study of Rathor history.
    Nensi was an administrator for Maharaja Jaswant Singh, the
    ruler of Marwar. He served both as a military commander and
    as a prime minister under Jaswant and had access to many
    documents that are lost to modern researchers.
Vir Bhan. *Raj Rupak.* Edited by Ram Karan Asopa. Varanasi:
    Nagai Pracharini Subha, 1942. Vir Bhan, the author of this
    eighteenth-century Rajasthani poem, served as court poet to
    Maharaja Abhai Singh, the ruler of Marwar from 1724 to
    1749.

European

Bernier, Francois. *Travels in the Moghul Empire, 1658–1668.*
    Translated by Archibald Constable and revised by Vincent A.
    Smith. 2d ed. London: Oxford University Press, 1916.
Finch, William. *The Travels of William Finch, 1608–11.* Edited
    by William Foster. London: Oxford University Press, 1921.
Manucci, Niccolo. *Storia Do Mogor or Mogul India.* Translated
    by William Irvine. London: Murray, 1906–1908. Manucci
    was a Venetian adventurer who spent more than fifty years
    in the subcontinent. His account of India in the last half of
    the seventeenth century is entertaining but not very reliable
    as a historical source.
Mundy, Peter. *Travels in Asia, 1630–34.* Edited by R. C. Temple.
    Hakluyt Society. 2d Series, vol. 35. London: Oxford Uni-
    versity Press, 1914.
Roe, Sir Thomas. *The Embassy of Sir Thomas Roe to India.*
    Edited by William Foster. London: Oxford University Press,
    1926. Roe was the first English ambassador to the Mughal

court. He attended Emperor Jahangir in Ajmer from 1615
to 1618.
Tavernier, Jean Baptist. *Les Six Voyages de J. B. Tavernier . . . en
Turquie, en Perse et aux Indes*. Vol 2. Paris: 1676. Tavernier
was a Frenchman who visited India in 1640. He was a jeweler
and very concerned with commercial activity in the Mughal
empire.

Secondary Sources

Books

English

Abd al-Wali, Maulavi. *Aurangzeb's Relations with Rajputs, Mar-
hattas and Others*. 1925.
Adams, Archibald. *The Western Rajputana States: A Medico-
Topographical and General Account of Marwar, Sirohi, Jai-
salmir*. London: Junior Army and Navy Stores, 1899.
Ahluwalia, Manjut Singh. *Studies in Medieval Rajasthan History*.
Aligarh, India: Aligarh Muslim University Press, 1970.
Ali, M. Athar. *The Mughal Nobility under Aurangzeb*. New
Delhi: Asia Publishing House, 1966.
Ali, Sadiq. *A Vindication of Aurangzeb*. Calcutta: Rahman, 1918.
Aziz, A. *The Mansabdari System and the Mughal Army*. Delhi:
Chand, 1971.
Banerjee, Anil Chandra. *Lectures on Rajput History*. Calcutta:
Mukhopadhyay, 1962.
————. *Medieval Studies*. Calcutta: Mukhopadhyay, 1962.
Bhargava, V. S. *Marwar and the Mughal Emperors*. Delhi: Mun-
shiram Manoharlal, 1966.
Bilimoria, J. H. *Letters of Aurangzebe*. Bombay: Taraporevala,
1916.
Bingley, A. H. *Rajputs*. Simla, India: Government Printing Of-
fice, 1899.
Birdwood, George. *The Rajputs in the History of Hindustan*.
London: Clowes, 1912.
Carstairs, Morris B. *The Twice-Born*. London: Hogarth Press,
1967.
Chandra, Satish. *Parties and Politics at the Mughal Court, 1707–
40*. Aligarh: University Press, 1959.
Chatterjee, Anjoli. *Bengal in the Reign of Aurangzeb*. Calcutta:
Progress, 1967.

Chauhan, Brij Lal. *A Rajasthan Village*. New Delhi: Vir, 1967.

Chopra, Pran Nath. *Some Aspects of Society and Culture During the Mughal Age, 1526–1707*. Agra: Agarwala, 1955.

Cole, B. L. *Rajputana Classes*. Simla, India: Monotype Press, 1922.

Crooke, W. *The Northeastern Provinces of India*. London: Methuen, 1897.

Desai, Mahendra D. *Hasteda: Economic Life in a Rajasthan Village*. Vidyanagar, India: Charotar, 1966.

Dixon, C. J. *Sketch of Mairwara*. London: Smith Elder and Co., 1850.

Edwards, S. M., and Garrett, H. L. G. *Mughal Rule in India*. London: Oxford University Press, 1930.

Erskine, K. D., comp. *Rajputana Gazetter—Mewar Residency II-A (1908)*. Ajmer, India: Scottish Mission Board, 1908.

Faruki, Zahiraddin. *Aurangzeb and His Times*. Bombay: Taraporevala, 1935.

Foster, William, ed. *The English Factories in India, 1646–50*. London: Oxford University Press, 1914.

Fox, Richard G. *Kin, Clan, Raja, and Rule*. Berkeley: University of California Press, 1971.

Ghauri, Iftikhar Ahmad. *War of Succession Between the Sons of Shah Jahan, 1657–58*. Lahore, India: United, 1964.

Goswamy, B. N., and Grewal, J. S. *The Mughal and Sikh Rulers and the Vaishnavas of Pindori*. Simla, India: Indian Institute of Advanced Studies, 1969.

———. *The Mughals and the Jogis of Jakhbar*. Simla, India: Indian Institute of Advanced Studies, 1967.

Gupta, Krishna Swaroop. *Industrial Structure of India During the Medieval Period*. Delhi: Chand, 1970.

———. *Mewar and Maratha Relations, 1735–1818*. Delhi: Chand, 1971.

Habib, Irfan. *Agrarian System of Mughal India, 1556–1707*. New York: Asia Publishing House, 1963.

Habib, Mohammad. *Some Aspects of the Foundation of the Delhi Sultinate*. Delhi: Kalamkar, 1966.

Hasan, Ibn. *Central Structure of the Mughal Empire*. London: Oxford University Press, 1936.

Hasan, Mohibbul. *Historians of Medieval India*. Meerut, India: Munakshi Prakashan, 1968.

Hutton, J. H. *Caste in India: Its Nature, Function, and Origins*. Cambridge: Cambridge University Press, 1946.

Irvine, R. H. *An Account of the General and Medical Topography of Ajmer*. Calcutta: 1841.

Irvine, William. *The Army of the Indian Moghuls*. New Delhi: Eurasian Publishing House, 1962.

Jaffar, S. M. *Mughal Empire from Babar to Aurangzeb*. Peshawar, India: Sadiq Khan, 1936.

————. *Some Cultural Aspects of Muslim Rule in India*. Peshawar, India: Sadiq Khan, 1939.

Jain, B. S. *Administration of Justice in Seventeenth Century India*. Delhi: Metropolitan, 1970.

Karandikar, Maheshwar. *Islam in India's Transition to Modernity*. Bombay: Longmans, 1968.

Karve, Irawati. *Kinship Organization in India*. Bombay: Asia Publishing House, 1965.

Katiyar, T. S. *Social Life in Rajasthan: A Case Study*. Allahabad, India: Kitab Mahal, 1964.

Keene, H. G. *The Fall of the Moghul Empire*. Delhi: Chand, 1971.

————. *History of India from Earliest Times to the Twentieth Century*. Edinburgh: Grant, 1915.

————. *Sketch History of Hindustan from the First Muslim Conquest to the Fall of the Mughal Empire*. London: Allen, 1885.

Kennedy, Pringle. *A History of the Great Moghuls*. Calcutta: Thacker, 1905.

Khadagawat, N. R. *A Descriptive List of the Vakil Reports Addressed to the Rulers of Jaipur*. Vol. 1. *Persian*. Bikaner, India: Government Press, 1967.

Khan, Yusuf. *Documents of Aurangzeb's Reign*. Hyderabad, India: Government of Andra Pradesh, 1958.

Khosla, R. P. *The Mughal Kingship and Nobility*. Allahabad, India: Indian Press, 1934.

Kulshreshtha, S. S. *The Development of Trade and Industry Under the Mughals, 1526–1707*. Allahabad, India: Kitab Mahal, 1964.

Lane-Poole, Stanley. *Aurangzeb and the Decay of the Mughal Empire*. Delhi: Chand, 1964.

————. *History of the Mughal Emperors of Hindustan*. London: Constable, 1893.

————. *Medieval India Under Mohammedan Rule*. London: Unwin, 1903.

Lanka, Sundaram. *Mughal Land Revenue System*. Surrey, India: Basheer Muslim Library, 1929.

Lyall, Alfred C. *Asiatic Studies.* London: Murray, 1882.
Majumdar, D. N. *Races and Cultures of India.* Bombay: Asia Publishing House, 1958.
Majumdar, R. C.; Raychaudhuri, H. C.; and Datta, Kalikinkar. *An Advanced History of India.* New York: St. Martins, 1967.
Mayer, Adrian C. *Caste and Kinship in Central India.* Berkeley: University of California Press, 1960.
Minturn, Leigh, and Hitchcock, J. *The Rajputs of Khalapur, India.* New York: Wiley, 1966.
Misra, V. C. *Geography of Rajasthan.* New Delhi: National Book Trust, 1967.
Moreland, William H. *India at the Death of Akbar.* London: Oxford University Press, 1920.
Mujeeb, Mohammed. *The Indian Muslims.* London: Allen and Unwin, 1967.
Orme, Robert. *Historical Fragments of the Moghul Empire, of the Morattoes, and of the English Concerns in Indostan.* London: Nourse, 1782.
Owen, Sydney J. *The Fall of the Moghul Empire.* London: Oxford University Press, 1912.
Pagdi, Setumadhava Rao. *Lectures and Maratha-Mughal Relations, 1680–1707.* Nagpur, India: Nagpur University Press, 1966.
Pant, D. *Commercial Policies of the Mughals.* Bombay: Taraporevala, 1930.
Parihar, G. R. *Marwar and the Marathas, 1724–1843.* Jodhpur, India: Hindi Sahitiya Mandir, 1968.
Prasad, Ram Chandra. *Early English Travelers in India.* Delhi: Motilal Benarsidas, 1965.
Rama-Karana, Vidyaratna. *History of the Rathors.* 1925.
Reu, B. N. *Glories of Marwar and the Glorious Rathors.* Jodhpur, India: Archeological Department, 1948.
———. *Rathor Durga Das.* Jodhpur, India: Archeological Department. 1948.
Risley, Herbert H. *People of India.* London: Thacker, 1915.
Rizvi, Saiyid Athar Abbas. *Muslim Revivalist Movements in Northern India.* Agra, India: Agra University, 1965.
Sahay, Binode Kumar. *Education and Learning Under the Mughals, 1526–1707.* Bombay: New Literature Publishing Company, 1968.
Sangar, S. P. *Crime and Punishment in Mughal India.* Delhi: Sterling, 1967.

Saran, Parmatma. *Provincial Government of the Mughals, 1526–1658*. Allahabad, India: Kitabistan, 1941.

———. *Studies on Medieval Indian History*. Delhi: Ranjit Publishers, 1952.

Sarda, D. B. *Ajmer: Historical and Descriptive*. Ajmer, India: Fine Arts Press, 1941.

Sarkar, Jadunath. *Fall of the Mughal Empire*. Calcutta: Sarkar, 1932.

———. *A History of Aurangzeb*. 3 vols. Calcutta: Sarkar, 1925.

———. *The House of Shivaji*. Calcutta: Chatterjee, 1955.

———. *The India of Aurangzeb*. Calcutta: Bose, 1902.

———. *Maratha Family Records of the Seventeenth Century*. Calcutta: Indian Historical Records Commission, 1927.

———. *Military History of India*. Calcutta: Sarkar, 1960.

———. *A Short History of Aurangzeb, 1618–1707*. London: Longmans, 1930.

———. *Studies in Mughal India*. Calcutta: Sarkar, 1919.

Sarkar, Jagadish Narayan. *The Life of Mir Jumla*. Calcutta: Thacker, Spink, 1951.

Sharma, Dasharatha. *Lectures on Rajput History and Culture*. Delhi: Motilal Benarsidas, 1970.

Sharma, G. N. *Mewar and the Mughal Emperors*. Agra, India: Agarwala, 1962.

———. *Rajasthan Studies*. Agra, India: Lakshmi Agarwala, 1970.

———. *Social Life in Medieval Rajasthan*. Agra, India: Agarwala, 1962.

Sharma, Mathura Lal. *History of the Jaipur State*. Jaipur, India: Rajasthan Institute of Historical Research, 1969.

Sharma, Ram. *The Making of Modern India*. Bombay: Oriental Longmans, 1951.

Sharma, S. R. *Maratha History Re-examined, 1295–1707*. Bombay: Karnath, 1944.

———. *Mughal Empire in India*. Agra, India: Agarwala, 1966.

———. *Mughal Government and Administration*. Bombay: Hind Kitabs, 1951.

———. *The Religious Policies of the Mughal Emperors*. Bombay: Asia Publishing House, 1962.

Shastri, Shobhalal. *Chittorgarh*. Udaipur, India: State Printing Press, 1928.

Sherwani, Haroon Khan. *Cultural Trends in Medieval India*. Bombay: Asia Publishing House, 1969.

Showers, H. L. *Notes on Jaipur*. Jaipur, India: 1909.

Spear, Percival. *A History of India.* Vol. 2. Baltimore: Pelican, 1968.

Srivastava, A. L. *The History of India.* Agra, India: Agarwala, 1964.

Thorner, Daniel. "Feudalism in India." In *Feudalism in History,* edited by Rushton Coulborn. Princeton: Princeton University Press, 1956.

Tod, James. *Annals and Antiquities of Rajputana.* Edited by William Crooke. 3 vols. London: Oxford University Press, 1920.

Varma, Ramesh Chandra. *Foreign Policy of the Great Moghuls.* Agra, India: Agarwala, 1967.

Veeraraghavan, V. *The Great Heroes of Rajasthan.* Tenali, India: Jaya Publishers, 1949.

Von Furer-Haimendorf, C. "The Historical Value of Indian Bardic Literature." In *Historians of India, Pakistan and Ceylon,* edited by C. H. Philips. London: Oxford University Press, 1961.

Vyas, R. P. *Role of Nobility in Marwar, 1800–73.* New Delhi: Jain, 1969.

Yasin, Mohammed. *A Social History of Islamic India, 1605–1748.* Lucknow, India: Upper India Publishing House, 1958.

Hindi

Cundavata, Lakshmi. *Gira Unca, Unca Garham.* Jaipur, India: Rajasthan Sanskrit Parishad, 1966.

Das, Kaviraja Shyamal. *Vir Vinod.* 3 vols. Udaipur, India: 1898.

Dashora, Jamana Lal. *Rajasthana ka Samikshatomaka Bhugola.* Udaipur, India: Ramesh Book Store, 1968.

Gahlot, Jagadish Singh. *Aitihasika Lekhamala.* Jodhpur, India: Hindi Sahitya Mandir, 1969.

———. *Mewara Rajya va Kendriva Saktiyam.* Jodhpur, India: Hindi Sahitya Mandir, 1966.

———. *Rajputana ka Itihasa.* Jodhpur, India: Hindi Sahitya Mandir, 1960.

———. *Vira Durgadas Rathaur.* Jodhpur, India: Hindi Sahitya Mandir, 1966.

Gahlot, Sukhvir Singh. *Rajasthana ka Sankshipta Itihasa.* Jaipur, India: Grumukh Vitruk Champala Ranks, 1969.

———. *Rajasthana ke Ithihasa ka Tithikrama.* Jodhpur, India: Hindi Sahitya Mandir, 1967.

Goyaliya, Ayodhya Prasad. *Mughala Badasaomki Kohani Unaki Zabani.* Varanasi, India: Vishvabidhalya Prakashan, 1968.

————. *Rathauda Vamsha ri Vigata.* Jodhpur, India: Rajasthan Prachyavidh Pratishtan, 1968.

Mahesadasa, Rava. *Binhairasau.* Jodhpur, India: Rajasthan Prachyavidh Pratishtan, 1966.

Ojha. G. H. *Jodhpur Rajya ka Itihas.* 3 vols. Ajmer, India: 1938.

Prabhakara, Manohara, ed. *Rajasthani Sahitya aura Samkrti.* Jaipur, India: Asia Publishing House, 1965.

Reu, Bisheshwar Nath. *Marwar ka Itihas.* 3 vols. Jodhpur, India: 1938–1940.

Samar, Devilal. *Rajasthana ke Bhavai.* Udaipur, India: Indian Mandel, 1967.

Sekhavata, Saubhagyasimha. *Rajasthani Sahitya aura Itihasa.* Jodhpur, India: Rajasthani Shodh Sanstan, 1968.

Sharma, G. N. *Aitihasika Nibandha: Rajasthan.* Jodhpur, India: Hindi Sahitya Mandir, 1970.

Sharma, Mathura Lal. *Mugalakalina Bharata.* Gwalior, India: Kailish Pustak Sudun, 1970.

————. *Mugala Samrajaya ka Udaya auro Vaibhava.* Bhopal, India: Kailash Pustak Sadan, 1968.

————. *Mugala Samrajya ka Patana.* Bhopal, India: Kailash Pustak Sadan, 1968.

Somani, Ramvallabh. *Aitihasika Shoda Sangraha.* Jodhpur, India: Hindi Sahitya Mandir, 1970.

————. *Vira Bhumi Cittaura.* Jaipur, India: Vituruk Chumpalal Ranka, 1969.

Urdu

Abdurrahman, Sabahuddin. *Hindustan ke Musabman.* Azamgarh, India: Musannifin, 1963.

————. *Hindustan ke Salatin Ulama.* Azamgarh, India: Musannifin, 1964.

Ansari, Nurul Hasan. *Farsi Abad ba'ahd-i-Aurangzeb.* Delhi: Purshina, 1969.

Miyan, Sayyid M. *Shahan-i-Mugaliyah ki 'ahdmen.* Delhi: Mir, 1964.

Saran, P., ed. *Farsi Akhbarat o Maraslat.* Delhi: Government of India Archives, 1968.

Sayyid, M. M. *Omara-i-Hinood.* Kanpur, India: Khan, 1910.

Shibli, Numani. *Aurangzeb Alamgir.* Delhi: Sayeed, 1911.

Siddiqi, Abdul Majeed. *Tarikh-i-Hind-i'ahd-i-Vusta.* Hyderabad, India: Husain, 1967.

Siddiqi, Muhammud Sadiq Husain. *Tarikh-i-Hind*. Lucknow, India: Anjuman, 1966.

Articles

Agrawala, R. C. "Mandor—the Ancient Capital of Jodhpur," *March of India* 8 (February 1957):86–93.
———. "A Short Note on Two Unpublished Muslim Inscriptions from Rajasthan," *Journal of Bihar Research Institute* 42 (June 1956):103–9.
Ali, M. Athar. "Rathor Rebellion," *Proceedings of Indian History Conference, Aligarh Session* (December 1960):28–33.
Ansari, Mohammed Azher. "The Harem of the Great Moghals," *Islamic Culture* 34 (January 1960):1–13; (April 1960): 107–24.
Arasaratnam, S. "The Politics of Commerce in the Costal Regions of Tamil Nad 1650–1700," *South Asia*, no. 1 (1971):163–85.
Atal, Yogesh. "Short-Lived Alliances as an Aspect of Factionalism in an Indian Village," *Journal of the Social Sciences* 3 (1962): 65–75.
Baden-Powell, B. H. "Notes on the Origin of the Lunar and Solar Aryan Tribes and on the Rajput Clans," *Journal of the Royal Asiatic Society of Great Britain and Ireland* 31 (1899): 297–328.
Banerjee, Anil Chandra. "Expansion of the Rathor State in Marwar," *Indian Historical Quarterly* 28 (June 1952):215–26.
Bhandarkar, D. R. "The Guhilots," *Journal of the Asiatic Society of Bengal* 5 (1909):167–87.
Bose, A. B. "Rural Family Organization in Western Rajasthan," *Eastern Anthropologist* 19 (September–December 1966): 163–76.
Bose, A. B., and Jodha, N. S. "Ethnological Study of Village Abadi in Western Rajasthan," *Eastern Anthropologist* 21 (January–April 1968): 37–44.
Chandra, Janan. "Aurangzeb and the Hindu Temples," *Journal of Pakistan Historical Society* 5 (October 1957):276–80.
Chandra, Satish. "Some Aspects of the Growth of a Money Economy in India During the Seventeenth Century," *Indian Economic and Social History Review* 3 (December 1966): 321–31.
Chaudhauri, Nirad. "Rajput Songs of War," *Modern Review* 65 (January 1959):64–72; (February 1959):171–79.

Cole, B. L. "The Rajput Clans of Rajputana," *Census of India* 27 (1931). Meerut: Government of India, 1932.

Coulborn, Rushton. "Feudalism, Brahmanism and the Intrusion of Islam Upon Indian History," *Comparative Studies in Society and History* 10 (1968):357–74.

Crooke, William. "Rajputs and the Marathas," *Journal of the Royal Anthropological Institute* 40 (1910):39–48.

Cunnison, Ian. "History and Genealogies in a Conquest State," *American Anthropologist* 59 (1957):20–31.

Dave, T. N. "The Institution of Bards in Western India," *Eastern Anthropologist* 4 (March–August 1951):166–71.

Furber, Holden. "The Overland Route to India in the Seventeenth and Eighteenth Centuries," *Journal of Indian History* 40 (August 1951):163–75.

Gangoly, O. C. "Rajput History in Paintings," *March of India* 10 (June 1958):220–26.

Gardiner, Peter. "Dominance in India—A Reappraisal," *Contributions of Indian Sociology* n.s. 2 (1968):82–96.

Ghauri, Iftakhar Ahmad. "Ideological Factor in the Mughal War of Succession, 1657–58," *Journal of the Pakistan Historical Society* 8 (April 1960):97–120.

Graham, Gail Minault. "Akbar and Aurangzeb-Syncretism and Separation in Mughal India, A Reexamination," *Muslim World* (April 1969):83–96.

Grover, B. R. "Nature of Land Rights in Moghul India," *Indian Economic and Social History Review* 1 (July 1963):1–23.

Habib, Irfan. "Potentialities of Capitalism in the Economy of Mughal India," *Journal of Economic History* (March 1969):51–68.

Hameed-ud-Din. "The Lodhi Sultans and the Rajput States," *Journal of Indian History* 39 (August 1961):313–26.

Hendley, T. H. "The Rajputs and the History of Rajputana," *Journal of the Transactions of the Victoria Institute* 37 (1905):70–99.

Heron, A. M. "The Physiography of Rajputana," *Calcutta Geographic Review* (1938):1–13.

Jain, K. C. "History of Jaisalmer," *Indian Historical Quarterly* 39 (March 1963):13–20.

Kadri, A. H. "Routes and the Transport System of the Great Mughals," *Indian Geographical Journal* 22 (April–June 1947):65–72.

Mellor, E. W. "The Home of the Rajputs," *Journal of the Manchester Geographical Society* 30 (1915):105–24.

Misra, V. C. "Geographical Regions of Rajasthan," *Indian Journal of Geography* 1 (January 1966):23–29.

Mustafa, Khurshud. "Travel in Medieval India," *Medieval India Quarterly* 3 (January–April 1958):270–84.

Pande, Ram. "Jat-Rajput Relations," *Proceedings of the Indian Historical Congress*, 31st Session, Varanasi (1956): 64–72.

Pareek, N. K. "Kathodias of Rajasthan," *Modern Review* (July 1957):286–91.

Parihar, G. R. "The Political Impact of the Marathas on Marwar," *Quarterly Review of Historical Studies* 6 (1966–1967): 148–52.

Pathak, P. D. "Feudalism in Rajputana," *Bharatiya Vidya* 23 (1963):59–68.

Pearson, M. N. "Shivaji and the Decline of the Mughal Empire," *Journal of Asian Studies* 35 (February 1976):221–36.

Qaisan, A. "Shipbuilding in the Mughal Empire During the Seventeenth Century," *Indian Economic and Social History Review* 5 (June 1968):149–70.

Qanungo, K. R. "The Role of non-Rajputs in the History of Rajputana," *Modern Review* 10 (February 1957):105–16.

Rahim, M. A. "Emperor Aurangzeb's Annexation of Jodhpur and the Rajput Rebellion," *Journal of the Asiatic Society of Pakistan* 4 (April 1969):55–72.

Ray, N. "Origin of the Rajputs: The Nationality of the Gujaras," *Annals of the Bhandarkar Oriental Research Institute* 12 (1930):195–206.

Reu, B. N. "Rajputs," *Indian Culture* 3 (1936–1937):289–302.

Richards, J. F. "The Hyderabad Karnatik, 1687–1707," *Modern Asian Studies* 9 (April 1975):241–60.

———. "The Imperial Crisis in the Deccan," *Journal of Asian Studies* 35 (February 1976):237–56.

Rudolph, Susanne H. "The Political Modernization of an Indian Feudal Order: An Analysis of the Rajput Adaptation in Rajasthan," *Journal of Social Issues* 24 (1968):93–128.

———. "The Princely States of Rajputana: Ethic, Authority and Structure," *Indian Journal of Political Science* 24 (January–March 1963):14–32.

Sangar, S. P. "The Lot of the Agriculturist in Aurangzeb's Time," *Journal of Indian History* 47 (April 1967):245–54.

Saran, P. "The Feudal System of Rajputana," *Indian Culture* 13 (1946):73–78.

Sarkar, Jadunath. "A Flower of Rajput Chivalry—Darga Das Rathor," *Modern Review* 34 (July 1923):58–66.

————. "Letters of Shivaji," *Modern Review* 1 (January 1908):
    21–30.
————. "Mirza Rajah Jai Singh and Shivaji," *Journal of Indian
    History* 42 (April 1964):251–64.
————. "The Rajputs in the Mughal Empire," *Modern Review*
    57 (January 1930): 33–41.
————. "The Rajput Struggle for Independence (1679–1709),"
    Modern Review 17 (June 1915):389–97.
Satyarthi, Devandra. "Rajput Songs of War," *Modern Review* 65
    (December 1939):171–79.
Saxena, J. C. "Profile of a Village in a Semi-Arid Part of Rajas-
    than," *Eastern Anthropologist* 17 (January 1964):49–61.
Sharma, Ram. "Aurangzeb's Rebellion Against Shah Jahan,"
    Journal of Indian History 19 (April 1966):109–26.
————. "The System of Government in Marwar," *The Calcutta
    Review* 16 (1925):260–68.
Sharma, Sundari. "Aurangzeb's Attitude Toward Marwar After
    the Death of Jaswant Singh," *Quarterly Review of Historical
    Studies* 3 (1967–1968):95–98.
————. "Durga Das Rathor and His Relations With His Master
    Ajit Singh Rathor of Marwar," *Quarterly Review of Historical
    Studies* 4 (1968–1969):168–79.
Shyam, Radhey. "Honors, Ranks, and Titles Under the Great
    Mughals," *Islamic Culture* (April 1972):14–30.
Siddiqi, M. Z. "The Muhtasib Under Aurangzeb," *Medieval India
    Quarterly* 5 (1963):113–119.
Singh, R. P. "The Topography of Rajasthan," *Indian Geo-
    graphical Journal* 21 (October–December 1946):143–47;
    22 (January–March 1947):39–45.
Sinha, Surajit. "State Formation and Rajput Myth in Tribal
    Central India," *Man in India* 42 (January–March 1962):
    35–80.
Srivastava, A. L. "Akbar's Conquest of Rajasthan," *Journal of
    Indian History* 38 (August 1960):385–400.
————. "Some Problems of Medieval Indian History," *Quarterly
    Review of Historical Studies* 3 (1963–1964):168–71.
Tessitori, L. P. "Bardic and Historical Survey of Rajputana,"
    Journal of the Asiatic Society of Bengal 10 (1914):373–410.
————. "Progress Report on the Bardic and Historical Survey of
    Rajputana," *Journal of the Asiatic Society of Bengal* 12
    (August 1916):57–116; 13 (November 1917):195–252; 15
    (May 1919):5–79; 16 (March 1921):251–79.
Wills, C. U. "The Territorial System of the Rajput Kingdoms of

Medieval Chattigarh," *Journal and Proceedings of the Asiatic Society of Bengal* n.s. 15 (1919):197–262.

Woodcock, George. "The Rajputs, Sons of Kings," *History Today* 12 (October 1962):558–67.

Yashpal. "Origins of the Rajput War (1679–81)," *Indian Historical Quarterly* 17 (December 1941).430–41.

INDEX